NANCY LEÓN
CELIA LEÓN

BALBOA.PRESS
A DIVISION OF HAY HOUSE

Copyright © 2019 Nancy León; Celia León.

All rights reserved. No part of this book may be used or reproduced by any means, graphic, electronic, or mechanical, including photocopying, recording, taping or by any information storage retrieval system without the written permission of the author except in the case of brief quotations embodied in critical articles and reviews.

Balboa Press books may be ordered through booksellers or by contacting:

Balboa Press
A Division of Hay House
1663 Liberty Drive
Bloomington, IN 47403
www.balboapress.com
1 (877) 407-4847

Because of the dynamic nature of the Internet, any web addresses or links contained in this book may have changed since publication and may no longer be valid. The views expressed in this work are solely those of the author and do not necessarily reflect the views of the publisher, and the publisher hereby disclaims any responsibility for them.

The author of this book does not dispense medical advice or prescribe the use of any technique as a form of treatment for physical, emotional, or medical problems without the advice of a physician, either directly or indirectly. The intent of the author is only to offer information of a general nature to help you in your quest for emotional and spiritual well-being. In the event you use any of the information in this book for yourself, which is your constitutional right, the author and the publisher assume no responsibility for your actions.

Any people depicted in stock imagery provided by Getty Images are models, and such images are being used for illustrative purposes only.
Certain stock imagery © Getty Images.

Print information available on the last page.

ISBN: 978-1-9822-3990-9 (sc)
ISBN: 978-1-9822-3992-3 (hc)
ISBN: 978-1-9822-3991-6 (e)

Library of Congress Control Number: 2019920181

Balboa Press rev. date: 03/17/2020

Table of Contents

Melodías (Melodies) 1

A Veces (At Times) 19

De Colores (of Colors) 35

Mi Amor (My Love) 51

Te Quiero (I Love You) 69

Sentimiento (Feelings) 84

Mañanitas (Mornings) 99

Razones (Reasons) 117

A message from my Mother:

Listen. I want to tell you something about grief. You might be up one minute and down the next. Be patient. Every day will take care of itself.

> "A bird does not sing because it has an answer.
> It sings because it has a song."
> ~ Chinese Proverb

Melodías *(Melodies)*

Have you ever felt someone's eyes touch your soul and make you feel as if you were the single and most important reason for their existence? Ricky made me feel this way from the very first moment I saw him. I felt Ricky's indomitable spirit softly touch my soul from across a crowded room, and I noticed him instantly.

It was a Thursday night at Lechugas, a small Italian restaurant and lounge located on the corner of a quiet street on the Northern side of the city of Denver. Lechugas was a very old-fashioned establishment with a picturesque setting. They served the best little runts in the world; a dago dog with home-made sausage wrapped in dough much like a big pig in a blanket but better because they included awesome tasting chile peppers that when activated made your mouth water profusely. When you walked into Lechugas your eyes were immediately drawn to the small cabaret tables facing a rectangular stage. The interior was darker than what you would expect because of the age and architecture of the building. The tables were carefully arranged very close together like tiles in a mosaic which did not leave much room for walking around to mingle. The only thing missing from this picture was the typical red and white checkered picnic cloths that one would expect to drape the tabletops in a place like this. The lounge resembled Ricky Ricardo's Cuban Tropicana Club from the 1950's American TV series *I Love Lucy*, only Lechugas was Italian and not Cuban. The restaurant walls were donned with historical black and white photographs of musicians and entertainers from the late 1960's. One vintage photo in particular featured the five members of the legendary Rat Pack: Frank Sinatra, Dean Martin, Sammy Davis Jr., Peter Lawford and Joey Bishop standing in front of a 1967 Vegas Strip. The lounge was not extravagant or elegant by any means, but I thought it was acceptable for a casual night out during the work week. My friends begged to differ and rarely accompanied me to Lechugas. They did not particularly enjoy the place because to them it was the land of dinosaurs since "Old people go there and the place smells like Vicks." I liked it for that very reason. The place was familiar and comfortable where I could be with old friends from the neighborhood. Because my friends were with me, it was one of the only places where it felt like home.

Ricky was a member of Lechugas' "Rat Pack". His close buddies Michael, Gary, Frankie and the owner Chuck would congregate at Lechugas to talk shop. Together they would drink beer and have passionate conversations about the pro league and the legendary players in basketball, baseball and football. The corner of the bar was their man cave where they met about once a week. They laughed at each other's jokes, entertained each other with stories of machismo, and truly enjoyed life when they were hanging out in their cave. This time was priceless to them, even if it meant the fun would only be for a few hours.

Thursday was amateur night at Lechugas. Marti and Marie had just kicked off the evening karaoke. I was lucky enough to be selected as the first singer. Being the first singer of the night has its advantages. No one can compare the first singer to the previous singer because there is no previous singer. Also, the first singer on the call rotation is selected to sing more times throughout the night than the other singers. Most importantly, the first singer has the honor of singing two songs back-to-back to kick off the night's competition. I had an annoyingly long day at work and was prepared to release the walloping tension in my head that night at Lechugas. My goal was to make the base from the subwoofers burst through my voice, deafening my audience while alleviating my discomfort. I was out with a group of my close friends. It was almost eight o'clock and I had to go to work the next day. I specifically told my friend Kathy that I only wanted to be out for an hour. However, I knew I would stay past ten if necessary, just to sing my selection, "Dreams" by Stevie Nicks.

Suddenly, Marti yells into a microphone, "Let's get Nancy up here! Where's she at?" On Marti's cue the cheering squad at my table began to stand up one by one and applaud as if to request an encore even before I started to sing. They chanted my name as they clapped enthusiastically. I was the last one to stand. Totally embarrassed by their adolescent behavior, I found my courage and managed to walk onto the stage with poise and confidence. When I reached the DJ area, I turned toward my diehard fan club and thanked them for their overzealous introduction. I raised my hands and slowly motioned them to sit down. I was thrilled to be on stage but quickly got very agitated when the music took longer than expected to start. I responded to piercing glares from the people standing in the front row by gawking right back at them. I was eager to feel Stevie's music take control of my voice, and just then the music started.

The crowd in the front row finally began to sit down. Their once impersonal eyes faded into the audience leaving an aura of anticipation for the show to begin. When everyone was seated, I was clearly visible under the spotlight from any corner of the lounge. I was wearing torn Levi shorts and a white halter top with a red and black Michael Jordan baseball cap. My friend Gary would often tell me that I could make a baseball cap look good. I wore sandals with a low heal because I wanted my legs to appear longer than they actually were. I was far from the epitome of a hot babe, but I still looked good. I was cute, simple and undisputedly, unique.

I loved Stevie Nicks. She was the only female contemporary pop/rock artist whose music influenced me well past my teenage years. Stevie's lyrics inspired and guided me into my performance. The magnetic pulse of the music instantly revived my body and I allowed myself to flow freely in and out of each note. As my body rocked and swayed, every knot in my neck started to unravel. My hips moved perfectly in sync with the beat. I began to sing my favorite part of the song, "Players only love you when they're playing." As I sang, I turned my head slightly to the side as to give the audience a sultry look over my right shoulder. I glanced at the long hallway and past two square windows by the front area of the bar. That was when I first noticed him.

I lost my concentration when I saw Ricky and momentarily forgot the words to a song that I habitually recited since I was a teenager. My eyes desperately scanned the big screen that displayed the lyrics to try and find my place before the audience discovered what was happening. Ricky glided into the room like an eagle with strong wings fully extended. Determined to make me his prey, he swooped down and seemed to fly around me in circles. When he realized he caught my attention, Ricky flew away and landed near the end of the bar. He perched himself far back in the corner and ordered a Cuba Libre, what I later discovered was his signature drink of choice.

Ricky captivated me with his presence to the point where I had to know more. Ricky caught my attention and definitely knew I was trying to get his, but he refused to look directly at me. Instead, in a timid and shy sort of way, Ricky's eyes were fixed down at his drink, yet I noticed he was peeking over the rim of his glass to get a glimpse of me. He stood in a dimly lit corner of the bar like a beacon in the night. His charm was guiding me as I sang. Ricky was smiling. His dimples complemented his face handsomely. He was tall and muscular yet appeared adorably gentle like a great big teddy bear. I was enthralled with all of Ricky's stellar characteristics and unconsciously let them take over my stage. I was hypnotized by this man and fully engaged in the beauty of the moment unaware that my second selection started to play, "I Believe In You and Me" by Whitney Houston. I transitioned from the trance back into the song. The melody of this track was slower, thus enabling me to give Ricky a very sensual, private performance. As I serenaded him like a siren on our exclusive island, the precision of my body movements lured him into a web of enchantment. I demanded to have Ricky's undivided attention. I reached out in spirit past the smoke-filled room to capture what I had already claimed as mine. From the distance, I felt Ricky's eyes on me. I could sense him watching me in a daze as I continued to softly sing before him.

When the song ended the applause rumbled through the atmosphere as if the audience was urging me to sing another song. My friend Gary was very emotional and wiped away the tears from his eyes. He was touched by the performance I directed at Ricky especially since Gary had recently separated from his girlfriend. My groupies were much louder this time and when they all stood up, I was able to duck down and sneak off the stage. Mortified that I had just made a complete fool out of myself singing to a total stranger, I anxiously blended into the group at my table, swiftly sat down, and pretended I was not the singer on the stage just seconds ago. When Marti called the next singer, I had recovered back to being just another groupie in the bar. That was when my friend Kathy leaned toward me and whispered, "Don't look now, but that guy in the corner, the one with the big teeth, just sent you a drink." I instantly turned into driftwood and I wanted to float away through the back door. I sat frozen for a moment facing the wall in front of me looking bewildered and gazing outward at nothing. I thought to myself, oh my what did I do? This was only karaoke, but I was embarrassed and felt like a stripper ready to collect her next dollar bill from a lap dance she just performed.

Kathy, who was a few years older than me, loved to give me her "Dr. Phil" lecture. She assured me that she would handle the situation. She said she would call her waitress friend, Augusta, to our table and instruct her to give Ricky a message. Augusta had long straggly curls of blond hair that was over processed at the ends. Augusta was to tell Ricky that I already had a boyfriend. Further, Augusta was to make sure Ricky knew I was not interested in him and I did not want another drink! I thought Kathy's devious plan could be effective in getting rid of someone and potentially might work. I was almost ready to let her execute the plan and talk to Augusta. After all, I was not ready for a relationship, and all I wanted to do that night was hang out for a few hours. Although it was only a drink, I could not have anything more than that. Still, it was only a drink.

Then it happened! I had to look back at Ricky one more time. When I did, he bestowed his will on me. I grabbed Kathy's arm and pulled her back into her seat! I told her to wait. I was having second thoughts about her plan. This man was really good looking! I told Kathy, "No, you can't do that. He might be my husband someday." I changed the game plan and told Kathy to give her waitress friend a different message. Tell the guy with the big teeth that I said, "Thank you, I truly appreciate the drink; I was very parched from singing." Little did I realize how simple messages communicated among people in a singles bar who are drinking zealously can be easily distorted and translated into foul "bar lingo." Four shots of tequila can convert an Oxford educated orator into a rebel-rousing teenage thug who delights in disgusting and offensive language. In the same regard, bar lingo is a nomenclature for some people who long to expose the stand-up comedian in themselves and hunger for humor. Speaking bar lingo guarantees that not all will have the same interpretation. Some people will find the communication to be the funniest thing they ever heard, while others will find it quite repugnant.

Bar lingo after 10 P.M. from a waitress, who is herself pretty tipsy, has a distinctive vernacular that disregards proper English etiquette. What came out of Augusta's mouth was inappropriate to say the least. In a rough, raspy voice she yelled directly at Ricky so everyone around him could hear her, "Ricky! She wants to rock your boots!" Translation: I want to sleep with him. I did not hear what Augusta said, and yet I worried that something went terribly wrong in delivering the message when I saw Ricky look up at me. He seemed flabbergasted at being the recipient of such a message and nearly spit out his drink! Everyone around him started laughing. I could hear Augusta's hysterical laughing, infused with a smoker's dry cough, from across the bar. Ricky's friends turned toward him and gave him a high five as if to congratulate him for sealing the deal! Ricky watched Augusta walk back to my table. When she approached me, she was still laughing.

Augusta, placed one hand on her hip, twirled her drink tray in the air and said, "You're welcome," then tipped her head toward the right as if she was pointing to Ricky. I sat in my chair with a blank look on my face confused because I could still hear the laughter. What went wrong? I felt like a deer standing in the path of the headlights of an unyielding truck, but I had to do it again. I had to look up one more time at Ricky to try and determine what he was told by studying his expression. When the two of us reached out to each other our eyes locked. Ricky raised his Cuba Libre and tilted the top of the glass forward with a sweet gesture as if to say, "Cheers to you." He pointed to his cap-less head then pointed to the cap on my head and nodded in approval of the number 23. I pointed at my chest then pointed to his Jordan shirt and gave him two thumbs up in the air. We both were wearing our Michael Jordan gear and it was love at first sight.

I could finally breathe again and the redness in my face from being embarrassed was no longer noticeable. I was reassured and relieved that nothing bad was said. So, I smiled with the biggest grin on my face back at Ricky. I was in the highest spirits, ecstatic with joy, and grateful that Augusta told Ricky what I wanted him to hear. No longer ducking down in shame, I confidently sat straight up in my chair, tossed my hair over my shoulder and with a fully extended arm, I proudly raised my drink to the ceiling. My lips gingerly formed the words "Thank you" to convey to Ricky my affection and gratitude.

As I recall, it would be years before I found out what Augusta said in her bar lingo to Ricky that night.

Several months after I saw Ricky at Lechugas, I ran into him again at a sports bar in Lodo. "LoDo" is like an acronym or nickname that Denverites use when referring to Denver's Historical Lower Downtown District. LoDo is a blend of residential and commercial buildings, upscale but with a hint of ghetto, and is the city's prime area for sports entertainment. The eye candy of Denver for all sports fans is smack in the heart of the city with Coors Field, the Pepsi Center and Sports Authority Stadium (built across from the sacred grounds of the beloved Mile High Stadium). Whenever Ricky was in LoDo it was either to watch a Denver Bronco's away game or to attend a Sunday afternoon Colorado Rockies baseball game. Hanging out with the fellas was just an added perk.

One afternoon I saw Ricky in LoDo at a Sports Bar. He was out with his friend Gary. Gary happened to be my friend too. It was this mutual friend that brought me and Ricky together. That day, Gary invited me to hang out with him. Actually, Gary invited both Ricky and I without either of us knowing it. When I walked into to the bar, my eyes landed on Ricky and bypassed Gary altogether. Gary must have caught my reaction because he immediately grabbed my hand and told me, "I want you to meet someone." Gary placed my hand in Ricky's hand and said, "The two of you need to meet each other. Nancy this is Rick, Rick this is Nancy." The first thing I noticed when Ricky held my hand was that his hands were so soft and clean. Ricky was much taller than me, so I made him sit down on the stool next to the bar. The Denver Broncos were playing a home game against their division rivalry, the Oakland Raiders, and the game was on eight television screens scattered in front of us throughout the bar. For those who are not familiar with football fans or division rivalries, the Bronco-Raider rivalry is one of the most vehement and heated rivalries in the pro-football league. Ricky was a faithful Bronco fanatic and I loved the Raiders. They say that opposites attract. Well, one would think that after Ricky saw me in my Raiders gear, he would have had a change of heart about the rivalry. But opposites were not in my favor that day. Ricky got up from the stool and left the bar with me standing there holding his drink. I was engaged in a conversation with Ricky about the game when I told him that I slept with Jeff Hostetler. Hoss was a Raiders quarterback for four years. In the 1993 season, Hoss and the Raiders beat the Broncos 42-24 in a playoff victory win. Every Raider fan remembers this game where Hoss threw for an impressive 294 yards and three touchdowns. Hoss suffered a career-ending shoulder injury. Ricky thought I was joking about sleeping with Hoss. Then I made the mistake of taking off my jacket and displayed my #15 Hostetler Raiders jersey. I told Ricky about how "Jeffy," as I affectionately called him, was in the hospital injured badly and being his number one fan, I was at his side. That is when Ricky handed me his beer and left the bar. He did not even wait for me to finish the story about the night I slept with the Hoss; a night when I woke up in pain with a backache. I reached down to grab what was next to me and found a Jeff Hostetler bobble head lodged in my back in my bed! So, I really did sleep with Jeff Hostetler, if only his effigy in a molded plastic toy. I loved telling this story.

The crowd in the bar was a bit overwhelming and I had to escape. I set Ricky's beer down by Gary and I left. I should have waited because later I found out that Ricky did not leave because of my "Jeffy" story. He had only stepped out of the bar momentarily to feed his parking meter. After I left, Gary called me on Ricky's cell phone to tell me I left my jacket on the stool at the bar and asked if I would be coming back to get it. Ricky was in the background asking if I wanted to meet him the next day for lunch, and without hesitation I accepted.

I woke up early the next morning to do some badly needed yard work. I was not sure if Ricky would want to pick me up at my house or meet me somewhere. If Ricky picked me up at my house, I did not want him to see that I neglected my yard. Once I started working in the yard, I could not stop. I did not realize six hours had passed when I finally got a call from Ricky. Ricky was nearby. I had twenty minutes to get showered and meet him at the golf course club house and restaurant nine blocks from my house. Since I wore very little makeup and my hair was long enough that I could pull it up after I washed it, I could stay within the boundaries of my time restriction. The problem was that I did not have anything decent to wear that was washed and ironed except a pair of grey sweats. As it turned out, they were perfect. I threw a black wrap around my shoulders and no one could tell I dressed down. Actually, I looked pretty good and made it to the restaurant before Ricky.

I knew very little about Ricky and had tons of questions to ask him. I settled into a patio chair outside on the deck by the putting green and I waited, and waited, and waited. It finally occurred to me that Ricky was not coming, and I left in disappointment. As I was walking down the front steps of the restaurant, I looked over to the parking lot on my left and saw Ricky get out of his car. Ricky walked up to me and tenderly kissed me on the cheek. My disappointment disappeared. Ricky said he was getting ready to leave because he thought I stood him up. Ricky went on to tell me he was just thinking over and over to himself, "This girl has some balls, she stood me up!" That was the moment I knew Ricky would want to call the shots, tell me, direct me, and control me. A silent, yet blaring warning alarm sounded in my head. I immediately called out to my gargoyles to take a post on my imaginary security fence. Gargoyles were a mythical species of ambiguous gender from medieval times whose purpose was to confront chaos and danger. My Gargoyles would protect me from harm. I was on heightened alert and proceeded to go back into the golf course restaurant with all defensive, precautionary measures in place to protect my heart. Ricky and I sat down on the patio and ordered a few drinks. I shed the black wrap from my shoulders and placed it behind my chair. My arms looked evenly toned from working out in the yard all summer and Ricky noticed them right away. I asked Ricky, "Where are you from?" That was the first question and the beginning of a long conversation. With the sun radiating its energy on us and the crystals in the ice cubes sparkling in our cocktails, I relaxed in my chair as Ricky began to tell me a story about a small town where he grew up called Florence, Colorado.

Florence is nestled in the Rocky Mountain foothills about 100 miles south of Denver. The most notable feature of Florence is its special accommodations for those on a sabbatical leave from society, otherwise referred to as the high-security prison system of the Florence Federal Correction Complex. Within the complex is the United States Penitentiary Administrative Maximum Facility also known as the Supermax or Alcatraz of the Rockies. This maximum-security facility is home to men who are deemed the most dangerous to society, including spies, terrorists and threats to national security. Despite its connection with incarceration, Florence is a very small-town rich in history and culture inhabited by tight-niched families. The lifestyle in Florence makes you feel as if you are living at least thirty years in the past. Florence's Main Street could be the location of the old television series, *Mayberry R.F.D.* The buildings are simple, the side streets are not paved. The school doubles as the high school and the middle school. There is one church and one hotel.

Ricky talked about his life in Florence. He was raised by his maternal grandparents, Simon and Braulia. He talked about his youth, teenage and young adult years with an apprehension of visiting the past, but at the same time with a child's thrill of being able to share his story with someone listening intently to him. I heard stories of how Ricky would dance with his Grandmother early in the morning before he went to school. When Ricky's Grandmother wanted to dance, they danced regardless of the time of day. Ricky told me that he would try to run away from her, but his Grandma would catch him every time. They danced to Mariachi music echoing in the kitchen. When the song ended and the dance was over, Ricky would say his prayers and then he was finally free to run out the front door and start his day. Ricky worked at the Royal Gorge Bridge when he was a teenager. The Royal Gorge Bridge is a tourist attraction near Florence where one of the world's highest suspension bridges crosses more than one thousand feet above the Arkansas River. Ricky's job was to work on securing the cable lines and he would dangle from a cable over the bridge as if he were a spider hanging from a delicate silk fiber of its web.

Ricky's Stepfather, Max, was a sheriff in Florence and part of Ricky's authoritative posture came from Max. However, I was intrigued to learn that the roots of authority were instilled in Ricky by his Grandfather, Simon. I never met Simon him but saw photos of him that made him appear as a staunch looking man, very traditional and old-fashioned. Ricky's Grandfather, Simon was very much like my Father, Enrique. Both were stern patriarchs of their families. They could hold up their index finger, move it back and forth from left to right, and without speaking a word could communicate the message that would bring you to a halt, "NO!" These men had so much power in one finger.

I was swimming in Ricky's stories and did not notice the sun starting to take cover behind the Rocky Mountains. I realized that I had only asked one question, but Ricky's answer was fascinating and without end. Eventually, we said our goodbyes. I left the golf course club house not knowing when I would see Ricky again but absolutely looked forward to our next date.

Ricky's uncompromising dedication to strong principles no doubt came from his upbringing and manifested itself in a distinctive approval ritual. When he was processing what to think of you, he would make a "head nod" motion that would give you a feeling like you were being scanned for top secret clearance. The head nod motion consisted of a slight tilt of the head, an upward lift of the chin, and a simultaneous grin and a raised eyebrow. Ricky's head nod approval ritual was his own creation of a high-tech human body scanner, definitely state of the art and one of a kind. If you made it to the grin and raised eyebrow, you passed and received your clearance. If you did not pass, Ricky's eyebrow dropped slightly, and you had to be scanned a second time. If you failed that scan, that was really bad! If Ricky cleared his voice during the second scanning process, you could expect to be subjected to the "speech." Ricky's soft and subtle voice would become a thunderous roar. His face would transform right before your eyes into a piece of granite, hard and cold. If his face turned into stone and he sharply tilted his head to one side then "it was on," run and hide! Thankfully, I was never the recipient of a failed scan. Once when I was visiting Ricky at his home, I was a key witness to a very heated telephone call. The unfortunate person on the other end was sucked into the telephone from another state by a beam of angry red light. I heard just enough of the conversation to feel Ricky's rage. I left the room immediately taking the next exit on the left into the kitchen to avoid seeing a potential aftermath of his wrath.

The more time I spent with Ricky, the more I thought he was an undercover Federal Agent, a "Nark", or a CIA Agent. I could not quite figure it out, but I knew there had to be a secret passageway hidden somewhere in his life, and I was determined to find it. When Ricky told me that he owned a carpet cleaning business my initial thought was that it was a lie. I knew it was a cover-up! I would tap on the walls at his apartment in search of a secret door to a hidden room. I even suspected a secret entrance to a secret floor directly under his laundry basket, but I found nothing. I was insatiably curious to know more about Ricky, to find the road to his inner being, but he was holding me at a distance. I think he guarded his heart more than I guarded mine.

I started interrogating Ricky early in our relationship and continued the inquisitive questioning well into our time together. Ricky, innocently and willingly, spent countless hours answering my cross-examination questions. He had nothing to hide and I had everything to discover. Years later, I finally surrendered to the fact that Ricky was telling me the truth, so I did the honorable thing. I confessed, I thought he might have a hidden life and turned myself over to Ricky's authority. I was surprised that Ricky did not give me his failed scan head nod or coldstone transformation. Instead, Ricky just shut his eyes and kept shaking his head. I remember clenching my teeth, covered in my "blanky," sitting curled up on the corner of the couch. I peered over the top of the blanket with squinted eyes, so they were almost shut. I cautiously opened one eye and saw his expression. I saw a smile. It was the kind of smile that confirmed what I thought he was thinking, "Where does she come up with things like this?"

Every time I saw Ricky, I felt his spirit from across a crowded room. Ricky caught my eye because he was a vision of perfection. Ricky's strength and power emanated from his soft, subtle voice. When Ricky spoke, his voice was a musical note in tenor, sometimes base, and his words had a rippling effect that flowed through me and lingered in my head like a funnel of a soft white light. Ricky was a confident man and not the type to pursue anyone. He never exhibited the need to be loved and certainly did not seek approval from anyone. But that did not stop Ricky from admiring women, and he would proudly proclaim to have done very well in the women "arena." Ricky never solicited attention. When I would occasionally see him somewhere during the weekend, he was always standing off to the side, in a corner far away from the main arteries of the room. People were attracted to him. I was one of them. I enjoyed standing next to Ricky even if it was just for a few seconds because Ricky made me feel like I was a part of him, strong and confident. Yet, there was a peculiar shyness about Ricky, and he wore invisible body armor to protect this vulnerable quality. I truly felt that if genuine love could pierce the armor, Ricky would in return give a very special love that would be well worth the effort. Ultimately, I was successful. My love meant everything to him. I became a big part of Ricky's heart. I believe, I was the reason that Ricky existed in my life, there was a story to tell.

I remember the first time Ricky and I danced a slow dance. We had known each other for a few months and the attraction was growing. It was the first time I let a man lead me in a dance. I do not remember the song; I remember Ricky's heartbeat instead. His heartbeat was the melody that played for me that night as we danced, and it played in a flawless harmony with my heartbeat. I remember resting my head on his muscular chest. He smelled so good and I fell comfortably into his arms. No doubt, I was aligned perfectly with him because I wore the right size heel. Not accustomed to a high heel, I was clumsy and somehow managed to get my shoe stuck in Ricky's path so that Ricky's next step landed on my foot. The pressure of his foot was excruciating. Ricky noticed my pain and pulled me in closer to him. He held my hand in his, close to his face, tenderly rubbing my hand against his cheek as if it were the most magnificent feeling he had ever experienced. I could not only hear the melody of Ricky's heart; I could feel it circulate within me, invigorating my body and soul. I was illuminated by soft, colorful lights that reflected upward from the dance floor. With every turn and in every step, I felt his touch. Ricky put his cheek next to mine and our lips became very close to each other's. But our lips never touched. Then the feeling stopped. It was as if we managed to dance to the edge of a cliff. Ricky told me that he could not kiss me because he would not be able to stop. Perhaps, he was afraid of falling. The music ended. I smiled at Ricky and gracefully thanked him for the dance. As I twirled myself around to float off the dance floor I thought, "What just happened?" Ricky was right. I would not have been able to stop kissing him either.

Later that night a few of my friends who knew Ricky commented about how surprised they were that Ricky agreed to dance. They acted like they saw an apparition and witnessed a supernatural event when they saw Ricky dance with me. I knew that Ricky loved to dance because of the days back in Florence when he would dance with his Grandmother. Ricky thought dancing was beautiful and lived to dance. Dancing was an expression of love; just like when you wake up to a sunrise and say the first and most important greeting, "Buenos Días," to the person who loves you unconditionally. It is a magical moment when the melody of the song and the memory of the dance find a way to last a lifetime. The dance lasted forever because time stopped for us that night. It stopped for us to enjoy that magical moment and to feel its beauty seep into our inner cores. It was the perfect dance, and it was our only dance. For many years after the dance, Ricky and I would have other special moments, but they would be scattered over time. We let so much time come between us, and we allowed each other to take care of life's demands without questioning, "Where have you been?" or "What have you done?" Ricky was a bachelor in the purest sense. At times I felt as if I was invading his space, and at times Ricky clearly told me I was invading his space. If I wanted to be a part of his life, I had to follow his rules. This was unimaginable to me because I did not have any rules in my own life. I was free to do what I wanted to do at any given moment. I refused to live with rules.

Ricky was very protective of his space but more so of his heart. I learned to love Ricky's rules. In the beginning they were a game to me. I would try to obey Ricky's rules and he would watch over me like a lion watching over his pride and try to dominate me with his presence. One of his rules had to do with my possessions on his property. The first time I tried to leave something at his apartment, he found it, and before I was at the front door, he would give it back to me before I could leave. I turned this into a playful game of hide and seek. I would search for places to stash my personal items. Every time I thought I discovered a hiding place that would win the game, Ricky would still manage to give me my item before I left. There was no explanation for how Ricky found my silver earring tucked inside his sock that was rolled into a ball stuffed deep inside in his shoe which was packed in his gym bag. Leaving things behind was Ricky's number one rule, do not do it! He made sure I complied with this rule and never left anything behind. What Ricky did not realize was that before I would put any effort into obeying his rules, I would intentionally bend them just enough to make Ricky think about rewriting some of them. What I did not realize was that Ricky knew what I was doing. Ricky would catch me bending his rules, and when he caught me, he would give me the "speech." All of Ricky's speeches began with "First of all..." Initially, I found humor in his speeches. I would ask him what was "Second of all?" or mock him by counting, "Third of all" and "Fourth of all", etcetera, etcetera. As time passed, I got the message. I even embraced his rules. I knew that Ricky loved me so deeply that his rules were a profound expression of his love for me. Ricky wanted me to be more than a good person. He wanted me to be an extraordinary person and to know the difference. In time, I fell in love with Ricky's speeches, but they stopped. The speeches stopped because I started to follow Ricky's rules. Ricky's speeches became golden words of gospel about rules that evolved into the chapters of our life's story and allowed me to interact within the footprints of his soul.

I knew that Ricky and I were soul mates the first time I collapsed into his bed. I worked an entire weekend in Copper Mountain, and I was so tired and ready to drop. While driving home from the work location in the mountains, the only place I could think about was how wonderful it would be to sleep in Ricky's bed. I found this thought quite odd because I had never stepped into his bedroom and I definitely did not know anything about his bed. I was overjoyed when I found out Ricky owned a king sized bed! I remember walking into his place. I looked around a bit, walked directly to the bedroom, and I saw his bed. I found nirvana. Ricky had four pillows to catch me as I jumped into his bed without a second thought. I slept alone soundlessly for hours. Ricky was dumbfounded and did not know what to think. We had been acquaintances for over a year, talked on the phone, slow danced once, and now I was in his bed! I could tell he was not sure what to think about the situation because he kept walking toward the bedroom and leaving abruptly. He did not step into the room. Instead, he popped his head in the doorway to ascertain if I was breathing. When I caught Ricky staring at me, he asked if I was okay. After I replied affirmatively, he did an about face and marched out of the room. I probably sounded like Satan talking in my sleep and scared him. Still, Ricky monitored my breathing every fifteen minutes and after a few hours Ricky finally decided it was safe for him to cuddle up next to me.

That evening Ricky turned on the television in his room and we watched *The Wizard of Oz*. During the scene with the flying monkeys, I shielded my head in Ricky's chest as the frightened little girl within me surfaced. When the Wizard handed out the gifts to the Scarecrow, Lion and Tin Man, I whispered to Ricky to get ready for my favorite and best part of the movie. Then, the Tin Man was about to receive his gift. I told Ricky that before the Wizard gives the Tin Man his heart, the Wizard tells him, "A heart is not judged by how much you love, but by how much you are loved by others." This was the first time I felt the overwhelming sentimental and shy side in Ricky. His eyes were tear-glazed, and he laid his head on my shoulder. After the Wizard's speech, Ricky simply said, "That was nice." We continued to watch the movie and fully appreciate the moment when the Wizard gave the Tin Man his very own red shaped heart and it even ticked.

The night of Oz was the night the heart of my soul was touched by the heart of Ricky's soul. When the movie ended, I had to leave. Leaving Ricky that night was so hard to do. I said goodbye for an hour, holding on to every second in his presence. I looked around and memorized what he had in his room and where it was placed. I left my handprint in the air so Ricky could continue to feel me after I was gone. Ricky held the front door open for me and he leaned down to kiss me goodbye as I walked out into the shadow of the night. Step by step I walked farther away from him. When I was completely out of Ricky's sight, I heard the door close. Yet, I was still connected to him. Like *The Wizard of Oz* that night was a classic that became the most memorable night the two of us would share the rest of our lives. When I arrived at my car, I looked up at the third level of Ricky's apartment building and saw him standing on the deck watching me leave.

Knowing that Ricky was watching me from above made me feel better.

> "Each moment of time comes with a reminder
> that there are no guarantee of another one like it."
> Anonymous

A Veces *(At Times)*

Ricky and I let so much time slip by us without seeing each other. When we did manage to get together, we savored each second like savoring the last drop of a delicious vintage wine.

Ricky's business kept him very busy especially since his office was located in Colorado Springs, a city that was more than an hour's drive each way from his home. A good deal of Ricky's work stress was attributed to the commute which he did six days a week for at least ten years. I kept myself busy too. My primary and full time job dealt with administering donations for a large hospital foundation for children. When I was young and soon after I entered the workforce, I developed a special talent for computer systems and databases. I could create a computer program that would turn someone's vision into reality in a matter of minutes. I used my computer skills to convert concepts and ideas into tangible matter, something that could be seen and analyzed on a medium like a computer monitor or paper. I also had two children; a son, Kieko and daughter, KJ. Kieko was over 21 and was responsibly independent. My son only needed his Mother on certain occasions, like when he wanted to share his career aspirations as an Executive Chef and boast about his personal achievements. KJ on the other hand, was more demanding, and I catered to her whenever she said, "MOM!" Ricky never wanted to interfere with my parental responsibilities. He genuinely appreciated everything I had to do for KJ. Although Ricky never had the chance to get to know my children very well, he was content and even proud to see photos of my children on Facebook. Facebook permits infinite access to the social arena when individual schedules make it impossible to meet for an evening of socializing. Facebook was Ricky's entre to my entire family; elders, siblings, nieces and nephews, and their many, many children, a key feature of a traditional Mexican family. With little experience in the children arena, Ricky was somewhat overwhelmed with all the family he saw on Facebook and declared, "You're scaring me!"

I filled my plate with life's necessities but still hungered for the fruits of life that would make me whole. I decided to donate some of my time because I was curious to learn "different" things, albeit Ricky could not believe that my curiosity drove me to work for free. I started with short-term volunteer work at the Anchor Center for Blind Children, a small school at a beautiful facility located on what used to be the Denver Stapleton Airport until the airport was moved and the area redeveloped. The Anchor Center for Blind Children taught me how children see not with their eyes, but with their other senses; their hands, their ears, and their smell. I selected this organization for volunteer work because my niece, Ariana, was born with septo-optic dysplasia and was a student at the Center when she was one year old. I was privileged to work with the children who helped me to "see" a different world. The children played with their toys by listening to the sounds and feeling the unique textures and shapes. I was so amazed and inspired with these little babies that could walk through an open doorway without hesitation, without fear. It was because of my brief time at the Anchor Center for Blind Children that I too wanted to walk without fear in my life.

Shortly after I volunteered at the Anchor Center for Blind Children, I decided that it was time for me to face my greatest fear. My niece, Michelle, happened to come across a website one evening when she was eating dinner at home. It was a stroke of fate that she happened to come across the website just when I happened to acknowledge the need to face my greatest fear. The website was for the Office of the Medical Examiner, more commonly known as the Coroner's Office. The Coroner's Office was preparing for the 2008 Democratic National Convention (DNC) to be held in Denver, Colorado. The Coroner's Office was soliciting volunteers to help their organization during the DNC. They were looking to recruit volunteers outside of their agency who could quickly assemble and assist in the event of a mass fatality. This was the perfect opportunity for me to face my fear of death because death would be facing me so there would be no other recourse but to face it. I contacted the Coroner's Office and signed up to help their organization.

On my first day as a volunteer in the Coroner's Office, I was given a tour of the morgue. One of the investigators who worked at the Coroner's Office opened a freezer and I saw some of its temporary occupants. The smell was nauseating! When I went home that night, I took a long hot shower to wash away the stench. As I attempted to let the steam cleanse me, I cleared the water from my eyes and startled myself when I saw an arm rip through the shower curtain. I shook off my imagination and went to bed only to have nightmares of people waking up from the dead. Despite, the unwelcomed aftermath of my first day as a volunteer, I stayed in the program. My first "ride along" with an investigator from the Coroner's Office involved a call to pick up a man who died in a fire inside his motor home. I remember how terribly sad it was that someone who had lived alone was also alone when it was his time to go. It was heart-wrenching to know that this man died all by himself, without a human to lovingly stand beside him when his spirit left this world. That was my initial feeling when I saw the body of this man burned to a crisp.

I dedicated myself to this volunteer program because I was eager to learn. I wrote procedures regarding what to do and what not to do during a ride along. I used my inherent talent to build a volunteer database. I wanted to make sure that the computer program worked well and that people like me, with no experience, could immediately take action and find the next of kin for people that died alone. I was fascinated by the stories, causes and cases of each death. The Coroner's Office made me realize that death was a bigger part of life that I never realized existed in the realm of the living.

I learned about lacerations and blunt force trauma from an intern. The intern took the time to carefully explain things I did not understand and completely answered all of my questions knowing that I earnestly desired to make the volunteer program successful. I wanted to be an outstanding volunteer, the best volunteer that the office had. However, my primary objective was still to overcome my fear of death. Each time I left the Coroner's Office I called Ricky and fervently told him what I did, what I created, and what I accomplished. Without fail, Ricky would break into my story and express his own remark by saying, "And you worked for free?"

Ricky made his business off limits for my volunteer time and it took Ricky four years to agree to hire me as his "extra help." Ricky already had a right-hand man that worked on creating his customer database. Ricky stubbornly did not want my services even if they were free. It was a macho thing. Ricky trusted his friend because his friend was front and center in the office. Well, that front and center position is not always the position that should be trusted unconditionally, especially if the person in this position is not honest. "When the cat's away, the mice will play." If you give this person complete access to your database and more importantly, your money, this person should be watched carefully so as not to be tempted by personal greed. I warned Ricky that he should watch his bank account and told him he should let me set up reports to establish controls in his computer system, but Ricky assured me that all was well. Eventually, Ricky took note of what I told him because he started keeping a hawk's eye on his bank accounts and discovered that his money was indeed missing.

I learned that the right-hand thief was not the only problem Ricky had at his carpet cleaning business. Ricky had employees with poor work ethics to say the least. They wanted paychecks but would not show up to work. At times, Ricky struggled to pay his employees, but he would always pay them before he paid himself. Sometimes Ricky did not get a paycheck and yet, he had to do the work he paid someone else to do. I witnessed all of it. Ricky was also receiving telephone calls from the dreaded IRS. When times were tough and his business seemed to be on

Somos 4-life

the verge of falling apart, I was there ready and willing to help Ricky salvage the pieces and put them in order again. I took advantage of these times to give Ricky a few words of wisdom. "Look at the good things first." I explained to Ricky how he was gifted. Running a small business required an exceptionally strong and special person. Not just any ordinary person could make daily sacrifices to put a paycheck in another person's hands so they could put dinner on their table. I told Ricky that what he was doing was very honorable. I described how he helped his employees' children have fond memories of a plump, juicy turkey on their table Thanksgiving Day. Whenever Ricky hit a bump, and there were many bumps as a small business owner, he would take personal accountability and blame himself. I was heartbroken every time I watch him because Ricky was extremely harsh and unforgiving of himself in the role of a financial provider.

It was not easy for Ricky to share his life and business dreams with me. When he did, I embraced it and held his dreams safely in the confines of my love. I worked my way into his trust and into his computer database. Piece by piece, I wrote the backend source code and created the functionality of the application. I spent countless hours memorizing how bits of information were connected to create a more efficient operating system. It was finally time to demonstrate to Ricky "the future" and how I was going to take his business to the next level. I asked Ricky to sit down, opened a notebook, and with a grin of satisfaction, showed him a mock-up of his database. I referred to the mock-up as his new pair of Jordans! I gave the database a badly needed face lift and added life to it. To my surprise, I quickly found out that breaking in a new pair of Jordans was not as inviting as I thought when there was an obstinate attachment to the old Jordans. Ricky did not want a new pair of Jordans; he wanted his old database back.

Although I was not successful at implementing a new database, I was successful at imprinting my name and my work on another of Ricky's work applications. With Ricky's help and blessing I started work on an application where four times a year, I would download the Colorado No-Call List and scrub the customer telephone numbers in Ricky's database against this list. During the application development, I was treated to four Lone Star steak dinners. Ricky enjoyed eating at the Lone Star because they served frozen peach drinks. Ricky was a regular patron because the staff knew he liked to sit at the bar and watch the game while he ate his dinner. When he and I went to dinner I had other plans and counseled Ricky that we were working. I would take out my note paper and start asking questions. I asked the same question different ways because I wanted to test Ricky's answers to see if he was paying attention. I also wanted to be certain that I knew what functionality he required for his application. There were times Ricky would look over at me and stare for a moment before saying, "I already answered that question." But I was one step ahead of him and I would calmly reply, "I'm sorry, I must not have heard you. I was watching the game." I was so clever! I could use that excuse and every time Ricky heard me say, "I was watching a game" he would consider it legitimate and let me off the hook in an instant.

I built the application so it was flawless and operator-error proof, i.e. Ricky could not break it. I converted what it took Ricky to do in four days into a ten-minute automated program! I was so proud of myself and believed that of all the programs I created in my life, this was the one I could sell and have income. The idea even occurred to me that I could start a side business to assist small companies that needed the service but could not afford it. I remember the look on Ricky's face when I told him all you have to do is click on this button and your numbers will be scrubbed. He was so puzzled that I had to show him a diagram of how it all came together so he could trust that it worked properly. Ricky was awestruck. I was quickly promoted to Vice President of Internet Operations and got a thumb drive from Ricky. Ricky's data and his entire business traveled with me wherever I went, and I still worked for free!

On occasion, I received a few perks from Ricky's company like Club level seats to a Colorado Rockies baseball game. There was one condition to receiving a perk, Ricky had to come along. Ricky thought he had the best seats in the house whenever he sat in the Club level section at the Coors

Field ballpark. Once, I ruined an afternoon ball game for Ricky because I made the mistake of dressing in all black. The elevation of Denver is 5,280 feet or one mile, thus the nickname "Mile High City." That day I over heated and melted away under the Mile High City's sun. Ricky was more concerned about me than the game. He plucked me from my seat and whisked me to an indoor bar so that I could cool down. I loved going with Ricky to the baseball games. He was always so excited and would cheer for a home run as if he were ten years old. Ricky was able to escape when he was at the ballpark; he was able to break free from the stress of a business that regrettably haunted him.

Ricky's lowest low was when his office was burglarized and his laptop was stolen. The laptop contained his customer database. Without customer information readily available, the business was critically wounded and on life support. Ricky panicked. The thought of rebuilding his business drove Ricky to desperation. He would have to build his business from the very beginning and start all over from step one. Ricky knew exactly who burglarized his business but could not prove it. I remember calling him that night to check on him. He was on the phone with his Mother. Ricky called his Mother when he needed gentle guidance and turned to her for special prayers and sound advice. When Ricky called me back, he told me what had happened. I could feel him giving up. I could hear it in his voice. He wanted out of the business. It had no value to him any longer. For twenty minutes I wondered what I could do to help. Then I realized that I had made a copy of his database and saved all of the files he needed on my thumb drive. When I told Ricky that I could recover his database he could not believe it. He professed his love for me as he kept telling me over and over again that I saved his life. I grabbed a few items from my house and headed to Ricky's place at 9:30 P.M.

As I drove to Ricky's place the only thing on my mind was that I wanted something out of this rescue mission. I would call the shots as to what I wanted, but I had to determine what I wanted. I could have asked for anything that night. I am not a greedy person and usually treasure what

I am given. All the while, I kept asking myself what was it that I have wanted for years but had been so hard to get? Then I got it! I wanted to go to Florence, Colorado, and I wanted Ricky to take me there. When I pulled up to Ricky's place, he was waiting for me with the front door open. Before I handed over the goods, I told Ricky that I wanted three things from him. Ricky braced himself and told me, "Go ahead, ask... Everyone always asks for something." I said, "Number one, I want my software back after you load the program on your computer in your office." Ricky shook his head and agreed to my request and waited for me to continue. "Number two," I said while holding up my left index and middle finger, "I want to have one of your shirts so I can sleep in it at night when I am not with you." Ricky smiled and told me that request was easy, so he ran to his closet and came back with a new L.A. Lakers jersey. When Ricky dangled the jersey in front of me like a bullfighter dangling a red cape in front of a threatening bull, he declared that the jersey was one of his favorites. I was appalled! I told him that I did not want his Lakers jersey. I wanted a t-shirt in which I could sleep in. Ricky had a peculiar way of altering his t-shirts. He would meticulously cut the sleeves and the collar to make them fit looser. The altered t-shirts looked attractive on him because they magnified his physique. He questioned my request by asking, "You want a torn shirt over a new Lakers jersey? This is an L.A. Lakers jersey!" I nodded "yes" and then watched him go back into his room. He found an altered University of Colorado Buffaloes t-shirt on top of his bed, brought it to me and asked if that t-shirt would work. I held the t-shirt up in the air then pulled it to my heart and said, "This t-shirt is wonderful."

Ricky was anticipating the third and final request. I held up three fingers and told Ricky that there was absolutely no compromising my third request. He glared at me with undivided attention. Then I said it. "I want you to take me to see Florence!" Once again, I surprised him with my request and he remarked, "There is nothing in Florence. Why do you want to go there?" I told Ricky, "You are from Florence. I want to see where you are from and I want to make all your stories come to life." As promised and without compromise, Ricky said yes. I made him stick his right finger in his mouth and then pinky swear to it. At exactly 10:28 PM, Ricky's computer was fully functional. His database was recovered, loaded and ready to roll in the morning. That night after four years of walking into a single man's apartment and gathering up my stuff each time I left, I was finally able to have drawer space. Ricky told me that I could leave anything I wanted in my drawer, and he promised me that no one would touch it. I guess that was his way of confessing that he needed me.

Ricky told me he loved me, but he was very cautious about saying anything more than that. When he did mention his feelings, he used the analogy of sports. He asked me if he was the number one contender and boasted about defending his title or the Championship Belt (me). Or he would ask me if he should retire his jersey and display it for everyone to see. Retiring a jersey usually was a sign of leaving the game to pursue a new life. This was Ricky's way of wanting to know his place with me, retiring from bachelorhood to pursue a new life together was all that mattered to him. I found his roundabout ways cute, yet very odd at the same time.

I worked for Ricky for two years and still did not see Florence like he promised me. During these years we had an intermittent relationship. We spent so much time working that when I got to his home I just dropped to the floor. There were nights when Ricky was so tired, he would forget to kiss me goodnight. The worst times were the trips I traveled late at night miles across cities through weather and dense traffic, crying because I was going to Ricky's place to work. Gradually, things did start to get better because I was the mastermind behind a plan that would turn the business around. I was depleting the useless tactics and implementing progressive tools that enhanced customer service and quality while reducing resource time. I analyzed the broad scope of the business. Nothing escaped my critical eye. Things were starting to make sense and it was all working as planned.

What was not working was a relationship with Ricky. I was his business partner, but as a woman, I felt neglected and unappreciated. I did like the fact that I felt a real sense of accomplishment whenever I worked with Ricky. Regardless of my relationship needs, I decided the work accomplishments were enough to ask for more space in Ricky's apartment. I laid claim to the end of his glass coffee table and told him that space was my office. He was fine with it. I took over the doorknob in his room and told him I was going to hang my shirt there. He was fine with that too. I told him I was going to leave my pink women's care products in the bathroom. He was good with all of this.

Except for Thanksgiving Day in 2010, Ricky and I never spent the holidays together. Ricky surprised me by inviting me over to eat Thanksgiving dinner with him. My children had to work Thanksgiving Day and Ricky initially said he was going to eat dinner at his Mother's house. Since I thought I would be alone, I made plans to volunteer with a group from my church. I asked my son to make a pot of garlic mashed potatoes and some homemade ice cream. I took the pot of mashed potatoes to the place where the church group was serving dinner. Yikes! I was truly disgusted at what I saw. We ran out of serving space and had to combine some of the dishes that were almost empty. One volunteer grabbed my pot of homemade garlic mash potatoes and chucked them into a tray with instant mashed potatoes. The result looked like slop! To make matters worse, most of the volunteers were eating food from the kitchen area where we were supposed to serve it. After my shift was over, I gave thanks and grabbed my empty dishes and my ice cream. I headed to Ricky's place to have dinner with him. I did not know what to expect because normally when Ricky and I ate, we had two choices, order in or dine out. I remembered Ricky saying that he did not like to cook at his place because he disliked the smell of food. Since Ricky mentioned that he was going to his Mother's for dinner I thought he was going to bring leftovers and serve them to me. When I arrived, Ricky was already eating. He was so hungry he could not wait for me. As I walked in, he motioned me to the direction of the stove and told me to help myself. I put the homemade vanilla ice cream in the freezer then opened the stove. A bird was in the oven! Ricky actually cooked a turkey for me! It was the first and only full course dinner that Ricky prepared for me and it was very, very special.

I served my plate, sat down next to Ricky and waited for him to say grace. I waited and waited. Finally, I had to subtly make the request. I asked Ricky to please say whatever it was that he was thankful for, as I looked down at my food admiring what I was about to eat. Ricky said, "Nanc, your putting me on the spot! But because I love you, I will tell you that I can be thankful for a lot of things. I am alive and I have my health. I guess when I really think about it, the most important thing that I am thankful for... well... I'm thankful for you. Now eat up and enjoy your dinner before it gets cold." Ricky was so choked up he quickly stood up and walked away to grab another Pepsi from the fridge. I sat smiling and feeling grateful for Ricky's admission. My Thanksgiving dinner was superb. Ricky even made Pepsi taste good!

Gone was the business relationship with Ricky that I once thought was most important. Ricky began to treat me exactly how I wanted to be treated, but there was one thing missing. I needed to hear Ricky claim me as his. That night we went to bed a little early and cuddled in the comfort of each other's arms. We talked about the years we spent together, when and where it all began. Then Ricky mentioned work and said I was the Vice President of Internet Operations. I asked him what my title was with him personally. He could not answer my question. I thought after all these years and all of the time we spent together I still did not earn the right to be called his girlfriend? That night I did not know if I could continue to allow myself to be rejected and denied by the man I loved with all of my heart. I knew that when I left in the morning things would be different. I decided I would date and perhaps find someone to treat me the way I wanted Ricky to treat me.

The next morning when I left Ricky's place, his neighbor, Sue, was sitting on her couch. She opened her window and yelled out to me, "Are you leaving?" When I turned around to tell her yes, she interjected that Ricky must love me because I was always there for him. Sue was an older lady and a bit on the heavier side. She was the security system at his apartment complex. I could not sneak by her without her alarm sounding. Ricky would imitate her by saying in a deep, harsh sounding gruff voice, "What up Rick?" and we would both giggle because Ricky sounded exactly like Sue. As I walked to my car, I could not believe that Ricky's neighbor could see that we belonged together, but Ricky could not.

Ricky and I spent the rest of the 2010-2011 holiday season apart. We answered each other's telephone calls and amicably wished each other a wonderful holiday but never made plans to be together. I diligently jumped into my 2011 New Year's resolution list and started a workout program. A friend of mine offered me a free gym pass at his job and put me on a rigorous diet. I was making positive changes in my life and felt like I was approaching a significant crossroads with so much potential. I was amazed at how a simple, yet consistent exercise regime nourished every cell in my body and made me look and feel good. I started the New Year with more goals on my list than any previous New Year's resolutions list. I was determined to hold myself accountable for 2011 and make it the best year of my life! Ricky continued to call me, but now I hesitated to return his telephone calls. I still hurt from Thanksgiving and I did not want to hurt anymore. Although I was learning to have a life away from him, I knew I would have to see him at the end of January to scrub his numbers against the Colorado No Call List. When Ricky realized that he was losing me, he gave me his blessing and told me to be happy in my life. For the few days that he left me alone, I really missed him. I had known Ricky for so many years. I did not know if I could continue to see him four times a year to work with him. I documented the procedures on how to scrub the numbers so that I could train someone else in his office to take over my job. I decided I had to leave Ricky because my feelings for him were too intense. I would not have been able to see him without losing a part of me every time I left. Ricky felt the void too. When he realized I was going to totally remove myself from his life, he decided he could not survive without me. Ricky called me and asked if we could talk. He was not ready to give me up without discussing our feelings. I, on the other hand, was ready to give up because of my feelings.

I agreed to talk to Ricky and headed to his place. When I arrived at his door, Ricky pulled me into his arms and told me that I was the love of his life and he would do anything to get me back in his life. I melted into his arms. We immediately started talking. When Ricky and I opened our hearts our feelings for each other catapulted. We realized we were deeply in love with each other. We quickly dismissed whatever it was that was pulling us apart and gratefully acknowledged everything in our life that kept us together for so many years. Then we started forgiving each other for missing out on so much time. We were a cohesive team, but more importantly, we were soul mates. I loved everything about this man, who in my eyes was a vision of perfection. And he loved me so much more. After what seemed an eternity, Ricky finally told me what I wanted to hear. He had me sit down on the couch and then moved to sit down on the floor in front of me. In a very soft and sincere voice, Ricky said he could not do life without me and he placed his head in my lap. Ricky told me that he loved me and would do anything to get me back in his life, forever. I believed in him. Then, Ricky asked me to marry him. He promised that he would dedicate his all to our relationship and gave me his word that he would be the best husband I could ever want. I waited so long for this moment. Happy tears poured from my eyes and streamed down my cheeks. I was smiling ear-to-ear with excitement.

We set our wedding date for February 1, 2012 and talked about this pivotal date all the time. We had several business-related things to take care of before we could start looking for wedding rings. I posted a white board on the most visible wall at Ricky's apartment to help keep us focused on our goal. Our assigned duties were noted on yellow post-it pads then strategically positioned on the white board. One day the challenges of life lifted the tape from the four corners of the white poster board detailing our journey. Our vision slipped and fell to the floor in front of Ricky's feet.

Ricky considered this an omen that the mission was hopeless, and he would inevitably lose me. That day I could sense his defeat when he held me close. He looked directly into my eyes and said that he would marry me in a heartbeat if he could. I anxiously replied, "Okay, I'm ready. Let's do it." Ricky did not have a ring and asked me if I wanted to go with him to buy one. "No! We are going to make our wedding rings," I confidently told him. Then I gave Ricky the speech about obstacles in life and reminded him of the challenges we had successfully overcome. I lectured Ricky about our promise to each other that no matter what obstructed our path, we were going to keep moving forward. I explained that a ring was not going to stop me from marrying the love of my life right then and there. Ricky was so excited about making a ring, but he did not know where to begin. He grabbed a clothes hanger and looked at it for a while but tossed it to the floor. I was excited too and ran around opening kitchen drawers and looking through containers that were in the closet. We were determined to get married that night, so we were relentless in our search. I ran into the bedroom and hit the jackpot. I spotted a bag of rubber bands on the dresser. That was it, a band! I yelled out to Ricky, "I found rubber bands!" Just then Ricky yelled back, "I have aluminum foil!" It was perfect!

Ricky and I sat on the edge of the bed and started to make our wedding rings. There was more than just happiness that filled the room when we braided the rubber bands strands tightly together. There was a life bond of hopes and dreams in the joining of our lives. The aluminum foil was carefully rolled into a shiny diamond and we secured it directly in the center of my ring. Our wedding rings were beautiful. Now it was time to bless the rings. We went to the kitchen sink and turned on the water faucet. We held the rings in both of our hands and then placed our hands under the running water that we considered holy. We blessed our rings with the "holy water" and blessed our future together as man and wife. Next we needed an altar. I knew the perfect place. Ricky owned a crucifix that belonged to his Grandfather. The cross was simple yet sturdy and rugged, like the old rugged cross sung in the Christian hymn. The crucifix hung on the wall directly above his bed. It was the perfect altar for our wedding. I told Ricky that we had to sit directly underneath the cross, so we hopped on the bed, knelt before Jesus Christ, and exchanged our vows. We made a promise not to share but to give our life to each other. We did it! I married my Ricky. From that moment I knew we could triumph over anything as long as we had each other.

Every woman wants to be loved and feel loved. No doubt, every man wants this too. Ricky and I reached a point in our lives where we were touched by an Amazing Grace because we were loved, and we felt love. The love we felt for each other radiated from the depths of our souls. We were truly soul mates. The melody of our heartbeat played in a flawless harmony as if orchestrated to be one heartbeat; Ricky's beat was baritone; my beat was soprano. Together our harmonic hearts murmured a romantic melody with unspoken lyrics. Each letter of each word in the lyrics of our life was like magical twine spinning and turning into a golden lasso that would secure the bond of our life story.

In our relationship Ricky and I allowed ourselves to be teachers as well as students. We were perpetual students, learning everything we could about each other. We acknowledged that we were not perfect and came with fears, failures and faults, but this was acceptable because love should never keep a record of wrongs. We accepted our imperfections and believed that this was not a part of our character to be condemned but rather a part of the lessons we had to learn as we faced our challenges and obstacles on our journey. Our insight and awareness of the imperfection enabled us to access the secret vaults deep within each other's heart and in the process, we were able to forgive and be forgiven. I learned what Ricky liked and disliked, and Ricky learned the same about me. Ricky and I listened to each other's voices. When we did not like something, we were comfortable in asking the other, "Why?" Together we learned that to fully understand the word "hope" was to understand the meaning of the word "bad." We learned that a bad experience could have merit. We talked about our dreams and our future together. We believed in one another and we held on tight to our dreams, love and hope.

At times, Ricky and I did not have the perfect romance. Our relationship was no different from any other relationship that experienced the ups and struggled with the downs. But we turned our backs on greed, envy, and hatred. Because we faced our downs side by side, we were able to stand up together. We gave each other time, time that was so preciously valued. The love we shared nurtured us and as we grew stronger and wiser. We learned how to open the heart we shared and completely extend our love to each other as we dealt with all of the complexities of our journey on the final road that was going to connect our bond as man and wife. We walked on what we thought to be "our" crystal road. Our life together was not a like the yellow brick road from *The Wizard of Oz*. Instead, our life was a road that sparkled like diamonds from the love shining in our eyes. Along the way, we were suddenly faced with long winding turns, hazardous bends and trenches, and storms that left us both weary and exhausted. Through many trials and tribulations, we never laid down because we never gave up on "hope." Through our journey, Ricky and I believed that "our" life together could lead us to our very own Emerald City, provided we stayed together in good times and in bad.

Ricky told me we could reach our dreams and he made me promise him that no matter what happens, I must never give up on hope.

> "All these colors are like all the love I have known
> in my life and keep filling my heart."
> ~ "De Colores" (Mexican Folk Song)

De Colores *(of Colors)*

Soon after Ricky and I exchanged our wedding vows, our lives began to change in curious ways. I equate the change to being able to see color for the first time; that is, to recognize and truly appreciate the beauty that color bestows on its environment. Through bursts of black diamond sparkles from the love shining in my eyes, I was now seeing color in every aspect of my life. Even the intangible became colorful.

Nothing expresses color more vividly than flowers and when I was with Ricky, I started to adorn my hair with flowers to blend into their radiance. I created decorative combs made of delicate, fresh flowers as well as elaborate silk ones. I wore flowers of deep, bold colors and flowers of subtle pastels. My hair was usually pinned above the nape of my neck as this hairstyle guaranteed Ricky could easily plant his kisses where he desired. There were other hairstyles too. At times, I tucked a hair clip at eye level behind my left ear. The clip held my hair back so that my face was exposed. My favorite hairstyle was cascading spiral curls garnished with a fragrant hint of Gardenia and Plumeria. The least formal hairstyle reserved for washing dishes or preparing dinner was a twisted bun with some strands of hair breaking free that was quickly glamorized with a dash of daisies. Regardless of the size, shade or shape, flowers had a mystical way of intensifying the golden-brown highlights in my hair, accenting my cheekbones with a soft blush, and accentuating my entire face with a natural glow. Whenever I dressed my hair with flowers, it was a clear warning to other suitors to beware my husband is near! The floral blooms communicated a secret language of love and gave me a seductive spark to capture Ricky's attention from his life-long dedication to watching sports. Miraculously, the television was silenced of screaming commentators and there were even a few times when Ricky turned off the television completely. I proudly became the most valuable player in Ricky's life, and he became my biggest fan. The life of a fifty-two-year-old bachelor was replaced by a very happily married man.

It was interesting to witness the transformation of Ricky's tenure with bachelorhood into married life. Ricky confidently guided me into the depth of his belief that our marriage would last for eternity. We established a ritual every night before we went to bed. Ricky promised me that he would be the very best husband. Then, he would fluff my pillows and tuck me in bed as if I was a royal highness and he my attendant. The sweetest and most treasured gesture of Ricky's love and affection was the gentle kiss on my forehead at the conclusion of the ritual. This special kiss unlocked the gates of my subconscious and delivered me to a rainbow of Princess dreams. Just as there was an evening ritual, there was also an everyday morning ritual. At the dawn of the early morning, just before my eye lids opened Ricky would passionately proclaim to the world, "I love my wife!" Somehow Ricky even arranged to have palomas appear outside our bedroom window in the morning, and they would gracefully serenade me. The Spanish word "paloma" is derived from the Latin word palumba for "dove." Although doves are white, doves are very colorful in a spiritual sense. A dove is the Christian symbol for the Holy Spirit of peace and purity. Perhaps the doves always appeared in the morning to bring me peace, but I neglected to open my heart and notice them. Or perhaps, the doves appeared because the intensity of my love was so energizing; love drew them to me. Regardless, these little creatures became a colorful part of my mornings bringing me their blessings each and every day. Before I could exit the front door to leave the house, Ricky required that I stand before him as if I had to ask for his permission to go. This was his unique way of giving me the benediction or blessing for my safe return home. The morning ritual was sealed with Ricky's kisses on my cheek.

During our brief married life together, I felt comfortably protected by Ricky's love, especially when we went our separate ways during the day. I felt the strength of his spirit on my shoulders guiding me as I drove. While driving, I scanned the radio and often heard songs that reminded me of Ricky so much, it made me feel as if Ricky was in the passenger seat next to me. Were the songs a coincidence because Ricky was often on my mind? Or was it because I was on Ricky's mind that he planted those songs for me to hear in my car as a way of letting me know he was near. Ricky and I came home to each other and that was the most important task in our life. There were no secrets between us. Ricky would listen to everything positive and negative that I had to say, and in return, I listened to him. He was so surprised at how open I allowed him to be.

Ricky was a strong man; he was pure muscle. He staunchly guided and guarded me. His love for me matched his physical strength in that his love was pure and powerful. While Ricky was always very solid, he stood over me like a mountain challenging me to never give up and climb higher and higher; we were going to reach our dream home and life together. Our relationship made Ricky smooth and polished like granite raised up in the highest heights from deep within the earth's core and processed to perfection to bring out the beauty of the texture, pattern and color of his love for me. Ricky grew into a magnificent force that glowed like a green aura around me everywhere I went. There was nowhere in the world that I could hide and not feel the love of this man. Ricky was the sustenance of my being. He made me realize that my happiness was worth more to him than anything else in the world, and he was bound to his commitment to keep the colors rich and plentiful in our relationship.

As Ricky's wife, my persona developed a new dynamic, colorful vitality. I became a reflection of colors; colors that you can not only see, but colors that you can feel. I discovered that colors can be playful and amusing.

I eagerly ventured back to the fond memories of my youth and shared treasured childhood moments with Ricky as if we were living them that day. Because I wanted life with Ricky to be confined to the temples of truth and purity, I returned to the innocence of a child prior to the inevitable corruption with adulthood. We fell into the grooves of our childhood when it was okay to uncontrollably giggle for no apparent reason. A time when we had endless energy to run outside and play and make mud pies just to be thrilled in the squishy feel of the mud dripping through our fingers; a time when it seemed magical to lie down on the cool green grass with arms wide open while gazing up at the endless blue sky wishing we could fly. I wanted to delete Ricky's stress from his carpet cleaning business and give him the opportunity to enjoy life. Under my guardianship, I was determined to give Ricky a new outlook on life, one that resonated in splendor. We were going freewheeling! Ricky was going to learn how to shake loose his burdens and free himself to laugh, have fun and make the most of each valuable second we so graciously were blessed to have. With a new outlook on life, we invented a new way of thinking and uncovered the answers to our questions by looking at a new world through a child's eyes. Nothing we learned mattered anymore. We tossed out conventional knowledge and defined our own purpose for which life was created. We developed our own theories about our universe, why our paths crossed, and why things were the way they were. Most importantly, we shifted our way of thinking to include everything around us because at every level, life was interconnected.

Ricky loved all sports ever since he was a child. So, it was natural for him to use sports anecdotes when talking about marriage. He said being married was like a series of really good games. There would be moments of triumph when holding the golden trophy from the victory win; and there would be moments of defeat when the loss would steal so much pride it was painful to return to the field. Unequivocally, it is at that precise moment of triumph or defeat when you realize the importance of having a life partner. The most inspirational feeling, as a child or as an adult, is having someone to run to when you are having a good or bad day, someone special with whom to share your life.

As a child, I loved animals and going to the zoo. So, it was natural for me to use animal anecdotes when talking about marriage. The striped pattern on a zebra is the most recognizable animal print. I thought marriage was like these distinctive zebra stripes. The stripes appear to run in strategic directions. When they run parallel to each other, the colors are in harmony and make a beautiful pattern. When the two colors blend in together life is in balance. Like the contrasts of black and white, life's journey is decorated in contrasts of good and bad, easy and difficult, happy and sad. I also think of a zebra pattern as the traditional colors of wedding garments. The bride wears white and the groom wears black during the marriage ceremony. These two colors contrast sharply but blend perfectly in the unity of a sacred system.

Ricky and I discovered that we both owned the same toy when we were children, a bright yellow rubber duckie! We agreed that rubber duckies were a staple that married couples, as well as children, should own. Ducks are an icon across the world. All ducks adapt extremely well to nature and are very sensitive to their surroundings. Ducks are diverse too. They can walk, swim and even fly! Symbolically, the rubber duckie represents freshness and cleanliness. When the lone rubber duckie is floating on the water in the tub, one can sense the calmness in solitude and silence by watching the duck move in circles around the tub. A marriage should be like this icon; a marriage should adapt, be diverse and always be cleansed so that love sparkles in a relationship. Ricky believed that I should always sparkle. In Celtic animal symbolism, ducks represent honesty, simplicity, resourcefulness and sensitivity. I think this is why I loved when Ricky selected the yellow rubber duckie curtains for the bathroom. It was by far one of Ricky's most simple yet sensitive décor decisions.

Ricky and I loved floating in and out of our childhood, sharing stories of our youth and making our present life more child-like and colorful.

When I was very young my Mother bought me a box of eight Crayola Crayons. I grasped all the colors; black, blue, brown, green, orange, red, violet and yellow tightly in my hands. I scribbled my name, circles and lines everywhere on a sheet of paper in my red Big Chief tablet. When Crayola marketed their box of sixty-four crayons, I was mesmerized by so many colors all contained in one box! Suddenly, I had no use for my measly box of eight crayons, so I tossed them out. As I grew older, I realized there were variations and shades of color when color is added and subtracted. If you mix dark pink with yellow you get red. Understanding color is by no means as simple as learning about the three primary colors red, blue and yellow which I had in my original box of eight colored crayons. To see color, you must have light. When light shines on an object some colors bounce off the object and others are absorbed by it. To have light you must be open to see the transformation in the shade of each color, pixel by pixel to reveal the personal beauty of an object that is presented to you. It is in the visual expression that you receive harmony in something that is so pleasing to the eye. Sometimes the most beautiful colors are obvious objects surrounding us in our daily lives but unfortunately, we do not allow our hearts to open and walk blindly past them.

Ricky and I enjoyed life's simple moments of time. We both had a lot of fun listening to a syndicated radio talk show on KOSI called, *Delilah After Dark*. KOSI was a commercial light rock radio station on an FM channel in Denver, Colorado. Delilah would offer solutions to a collection of love problems submitted by her listeners. Callers would hope for the chance to share their story with the super-breathy Delilah and dedicate a love song to someone. Delilah would ask the lucky caller about their love problem and the location from where they were calling. Once the dirty laundry was aired over the radio to the world, the caller could request and dedicate a song to the person that caused the love problem. Ricky and I were big fans of Delilah. We had our own comical interpretation of the show. Ricky pretended he co-hosted the show and provided commentary which usually alluded to the male callers not having bleeping "man-balls."

I would censor Ricky's commentary and bleep certain words, so it sounded like, "Baby you have bleep lack of bleep FA-e-e-lings bleep, bleep, bleep!"

Several nights Ricky and I stayed awake after midnight just to talk and make our waking hours together last a little bit longer, like chatterbox children who refused to go to sleep. One night, I told Ricky a story about a man I met years ago whose sincere words of love were so passionate that he made a permanent impression on my heart. The man's name was Flechazo. I met him long before I met Ricky. I was twenty-three at the time and Flechazo was well over eighty years old. I worked late one summer evening and stopped at a neighborhood bar for a quick drink. My friends Bob and Leo were leaving when I entered the bar. I chose to sit at the middle of the bar directly under a fan as the summer heat was unrelentingly inescapable. The stool was flimsy and as I sat, I had to concentrate on my balance to keep the stool from buckling under my weight. I ordered a Michelada, a beer with four shots of tomato juice, tabasco sauce, a splash of Worcestershire, a hint of soy sauce, and lots of limes and lemons. It is served in a tall frozen Mason jar topped with a salted rim. The bar was empty, making it easy for me to wind down and enjoy the quiet atmosphere. The bar was in East Denver, in a neighborhood that I imagined, could be a distant relative of New York's Harlem or Queens. There were two heavy black security bars over the front door of the bar in the shape of a big letter X. The door rattled every time someone entered. The rattling came from a bad paint job; the excess paint was rubbing against the door hinges. There was a small glass window on the door to see who was coming in and out. I used to tease my male friends that their wives were walking into the bar holding a broom stick and wearing hair curlers. Ironically, sometimes it was true. Seconds after the bartender plopped the Mason jar down in front of me, the bar door squeaked opened. I watched an older man stumble his way into the bar. He tilted forward as he shuffled into the bar slowly step by step. He had a slight hump in the upper area of his back and tried to stand as straight as possible. This man made his way over to where I was sitting.

He asked for my permission to take the seat next to me. I told him, "Yes, I would be honored."

The only background noise in the bar was coming from a dark corner. I looked over my right shoulder to see where the noise was coming from and saw two "regulars" shaking a vending machine trying to get it to relinquish some change or food. I glanced over at the man sitting next to me. We both shared a disgusted look on our faces. "So, what is your name?" I asked him. He told me his name was Flechazo and then he reached out his hand as if he wanted to shake my hand. When I placed my hand in his, he turned it slightly and lifted my hand to his lips and kissed it. He was definitely a gentleman and that made me smile. Flechazo told me that he just had dinner with his wife. After his dinner, he decided he did not want to stay at home, so he picked up his hat and started walking. He walked past the bar and then turned around because he felt like having a beer. Jokingly, I told him, "That's my pickup line!" Only Flechazo did not understand my joke. He went on to say that he never drank in his life; his wife never wanted him to drink. I was curious so I asked Flechazo, "Where is your wife?" Then, his eyes displayed the most heartbreaking sadness that I had ever seen. Flechazo told me that his wife had died a few months ago. He looked down sorrowfully at his full beer and told me that he really missed her. They were married over sixty-five years. He talked about how beautiful she was especially when she sat outside on the front porch of their home. She would sit on the steps of their front porch and comb her long silvery greying hair by gently running her fingers through it right after she washed it. Although his wife loved children, they were never able to have any children of their very own. She enjoyed having the neighborhood children play in their front yard. Now his life was painfully quiet without her.

Flechazo told me that every day since his wife died, he set the table with her dinner plate across from his where she used to sit. Every night Flechazo had his dinner with his wife. I did not know what to say to this man that would offer some comfort. His story intrigued me. I could not imagine having a love like this. I never knew a love like Flechazo's could even exist. I was utterly speechless and amazed at the significance of Flechazo's love for his wife. Before he left the bar, Flechazo told me goodbye and offered a few more words, "I loved her with my life!" Flechazo was overwhelmed with affection in his heart for this woman. The immense feeling when Flechazo proclaimed his love for his wife made me feel her presence through him. She never wanted him to drink and was tugging at his arm to take him back home. Flechazo's beer was still full when he left the bar. Flechazo left me with the desire to be loved like that. I would not settle for anything less. It was a privilege to meet Flechazo. During our conversation I asked him what his name meant in Spanish. He told me, "It means love at first sight." Ricky loved my story about Flechazo. Ricky told me that he would never do life without me and that he could love me the same way Flechazo loved his wife and I believed him.

As we painted our world with bright colors of our childhood and shared the sacred stories of our youth, Ricky decided it was time to for me to see Florence, Colorado. He became aware of how important it was for him to go back. Equally, it was important for me to bring life to his stories. I believe Ricky realized that the Polaroid memories he kept hidden for so many years had faded, and he needed to upgrade to digital memories that were fresh and vibrant. I was beyond excited. I could not wait to see the white house on the hill where Ricky was born and raised. Ricky's personal stories about his childhood memories were precious to me as they were like my own childhood memories. When Ricky talked about his past his descriptions were so vivid that I easily imagined being right there playing next to him. I could hear the roosters and goats. The laughter of family was the energy of love. I could even taste the dirt from the homemade mud pies! After many years and many reminders about the promise Ricky made with his pinky swear to take me to Florence, it was finally going to happen. However, the intent of our trip to Florence changed. Now there was a very specific reason we were going to Florence. Ricky decided it was time for me to meet his Mother. Ricky told me that during his younger, "rico suave" teenage years, he took many girls home to meet his Mother. She finally told him to stop! She only wanted to meet "the one!" This made it extra special for me. I was going to see Florence and I was "the one." I felt very lucky to have captured and tamed Ricky's heart, and I could not wait to meet his Mother.

Ricky gallantly decided he would be the driver during our trip to Florence. We hopped in the car, and Ricky carefully checked to see that I fastened my seat belt, and we were off to experience the long awaited adventure/travel package to the beautiful city of Florence; no, not the ancient wonders of Italy but colorful Colorado! The city consisted of only one stop light. Ricky warned me to keep my eyes open at all times or I could miss it. Ricky planned an "a la carte" tour guide for our journey. My questions had to stay within the menu selections Ricky prepared; which meant Ricky would do most of the talking. As we drove, Ricky spoke of many historical landmarks and cultural settings that I would see along the way. Every so often he would reach out to hold my hand and gently kiss it, as if to thank me for taking him back to Florence. He must have kissed my hand over one hundred times each way.

Our first landmark was the North American Aerospace Defense Command or NORAD located near the Blue Ridge Mountains in Fort Carson, Colorado. NORAD specializes in managing man-made objects. NORAD is a joint United States and Canadian Air Force command center responsible for detecting aircraft and space vehicles deemed a threat to continental airspace. Ricky claimed that one of the mountains by NORAD was man-made and there was an underground city below the mountain. We also passed roads leading to Pikes Peak, one of the most visited mountains in North America. The tip of Pikes Peak is above the timberline and reaches into the clouds. Pikes Peak inspired Katharine Lee Bates to write the famous poem, "America the Beautiful" and it truly was beautiful. Ricky could see this mountain from the box window in his Colorado Springs office. Driving along the highway, we saw roads that lead to the Cheyenne Mountain Zoo, a mountainside zoo, and Cripple

Creek, a gambling town that was once a gold seekers' community over one hundred years ago during the thriving gold rush days in Colorado. Ricky and I stopped when we got to the Arkansas River so we could get out of the car and feel the cool breeze coming from the river's rapid, raging waters. Then, we got back into the car and ventured up a mountain on a razor-sharp road called Skyline Drive that provided an absolute stunning backdrop view of Canyon City. Although the view was spectacular, the experience was hair-raising for me. After we reached the peak of Skyline Drive, I nudged at Ricky and told him I had one last fear of which he was not aware. I was deathly afraid of heights. I did manage to get out of the car, but when I looked down, all signs of being brave or courageous were gone with the wind. My complexion was Scarlett O'Hara white, and I was drenched in sweat. I sat on the ground on top of the mountain in the center of the road. It was easier to sit than stand given my legs were trembling. I feared falling off the side of the mountain. While crouched down and sitting in a squatting position, I felt a little more grounded with the earth. I exclaimed to Ricky that it would be better if I crawled down and meet him at the bottom. I felt a sudden urge to pray for my safety. Ricky was standing over me shocked that I could not even stand up on my own. He felt bad for not knowing that I was afraid of heights. Ricky lifted me up using all his strength as I was dead weight clinging to the earth. He assured me that I was safe with him and he would not let me go. After Ricky firmly lifted me up and held me in his arms, he slowly turned me around to face the scenic view. Together we stood on the mountain and admired the magnificent panoramic view of Canyon City. Standing on top of the mountain on Skyline Drive left me with the feeling of being above the world looking down on the intricacy and complexity of its habitat. Tucked safely inside Ricky's powerful arms, my fear of heights diminished.

We finally made it to the home of Ricky's Mother. My first impression of Esther was that she, like my Mother and like all Mothers, was beautiful and appeared to have a gentle and caring demeanor. As my Aunt Esther would say, "Esther" is an honorable name derived from a book in the Old Testament. According to the Bible, Esther was an orphan who rises from obscurity to become the Queen of Persia. Esther controlled the destiny of God's people, saving them from destruction by exposing a plot to defeat them. The book of Esther talks about the hand of God. A bad situation could ultimately be good under the control and watchful eye of God the Almighty. The Book of Esther says that if people would only surrender their hearts, they could learn of God's greater meaning. After my introduction to Ricky's Mother, Ricky mysteriously kept me under lock and key from communicating with his Mother. He specifically told his Mother that she was not permitted to have my telephone number. If Ricky's Mother wanted to talk to me she had to call Ricky first to get his prior approval. Esther and I could not understand Ricky's stubborn opposition to our freedom of speech. Ricky's Mother was forced to support her son's idiosyncrasy about exercising his right to private ownership of his wife. Ricky even built borders to separate her from talking to me. Reluctantly, we complied with Ricky's rules. That is, he thought we complied. Esther and I discovered a resourceful way to communicate with each other by using Ricky's cellular phone. Unbeknownst to Ricky, Esther and I talked regularly and used Ricky's cellular phone minutes to carry on the forbidden conversations. Learning more about the Book of Esther, I thought perhaps Ricky's intent to keep his Mother from me and me from his Mother was his way of teaching us a bigger lesson. Like the Book of Esther, we had to find the good in every situation, even the difficult ones. In difficult situations, Esther and I had to hold tight to our faith and to each other. Ricky wanted us to learn how to knock down barriers so that we would never become separated because as Ricky's wife, I would be his legacy. From the Book of Esther, I also learned that God has a purpose for us, and every person fits somewhere in His greater plan. God will even meet you wherever you are.

Ricky never had a chance to meet my Mother and although my Father died years before my relationship with Ricky, I felt a tender closeness with Ricky and my Father because they shared the same birth date, July 14th. I knew this day would be very special every year. In July of 2009, I started an annual tradition in tribute of my Father's birthday. My family gathered at my Mother's house for a ceremonial birthday balloon release in celebration of my Father's life. Ironically, my Father never liked to celebrate any holiday, let alone his birthday. I like to believe that my Father thinks differently when he looks down on his pride as we honor him. At the first annual balloon release our family had two women who were very pregnant with bellies that looked like big balloons. Since that first year, we have added a few more characters to the script, including the neighbor's spunky little girl named Ruby. The first balloon release was a source of comfort for us. Bright colored balloons were staged in the dining room. They drifted along the ceiling with colored ribbons extending from each balloon. The balloons were a vehicle to deliver personal messages to our patriarch as we attached handwritten notes to the strings prior to launching the balloons. At seven o'clock in the evening, we each grabbed a balloon and headed outdoors to the front of the house. Everyone held their balloon; toddlers, children, teenagers, adults young and old, and my Mother, the matriarch of the household. One by one, family by family, the balloons were released to the sky as the traditional Mexican classics, "Las Mañanitas" and "Cielito Lindo", sounded through the air. It was very inspirational to see all of the colorful balloons slowly rise together in the sky as they tended to float like a bouquet in the same direction. Each balloon lifted its special message to Heaven for express delivery to my Father on his special day.

On the third annual balloon release in 2011, a heavy rainstorm struck the city. Everyone worried that the helium balloons would not rise in the damp air. Kieko arrived early and wanted to release his balloon first since he had to return to work and could not wait for the others. Kieko wrote his message and attached it to a heart-shaped red balloon. He abruptly marched outside so a few of us followed. Then Kieko released his balloon. It did not float up but stayed at his eye level and appeared to look directly at him. It was as if the balloon was desperately trying to get his attention and tell him something before it was set free, but Kieko was not listening. Kieko was upset that his balloon did not lift off. He grabbed the balloon, reached into his pocket, pulled out a small pocketknife and started sawing at the string until he cut most of the string from the balloon. A gentle wind started to blow through the yard. The balloon was able to escape from the hands of the butcher and floated over Kieko's head, out of his reach. It did not get far before it got stuck in the neighbor's tree. Kieko started fussing and stormed off. He cursed all the way down the stairs and into his car. In the meantime, I ran to the neighbor's house and asked permission to access their yard so I could get the balloon out of their tree. By this time, my frustrated son already had his key in the ignition and zoomed away in a hurry. When I finally recovered the balloon, I asked my niece Elena to help me try to launch Kieko's balloon again. Elena was about four feet tall. Maybe her height was an important factor in how the balloon was released without an issue. I handed Elena the balloon. With her slender fingers holding the string, she gracefully released the balloon and up it went. Our eyes were fixed on the balloon as it floated higher and higher. Then, we noticed it. In front of the house was not one rainbow but a double rainbow painted against the discolored bluish-grey sky. Elena and I stood still like statuettes with our heads up, eyes back and mouths open wide. We watched the balloon in amazement. It was exciting! The balloon was graciously floating past each cloud as if to greet the clouds along its journey. I imagined the balloon informed the clouds that it was a special messenger delivering a very important message. The clouds parted, allowing the heart-shaped red balloon to head toward the rainbow. At last, Kieko's balloon dissipated into the colors of the rainbow. When the balloon was out of our sight, Elena and I finally showed subtle movement. We turned and looked at each other and said, "Did you see that? That was so cool!" I carefully recollected the details of the amazing journey of Kieko's balloon. Excited to tell Kieko about what he missed and what I witnessed, I dialed his cell phone. He was still upset but calmed down when I told him the story. I added my own message to the significance of the story by saying, "Sometimes it is within the final second after you give up hope and walk away that something spectacular happens. If you wait long enough, you will appreciate why you trusted your heart. You must always find patience within and try to hang in just a bit longer." There was silence on the other end of the cell phone and then a quick, "Thanks Mom, I have to get back to work... love you."

Inspired by what I had witnessed with Kieko's balloon, I wrote my personal note for my balloon. The message to my Father read:

Happy Birthday Daddy!
I want you to bless my relationship with Ricky.
Please give me a beautiful life with him so that
we can learn to love beyond love itself.
I miss you so much!
Love NaSadia

"NaSadia" was the nickname my Father gave me. He was the only one that called me this name and seemed to say it when I needed his guidance the most. Ricky tried to pronounce "NaSadia" but unsuccessfully pronounced it as Na-Sa-Dee-Ya.

Later that evening, I stopped at the store to pick up dinner and a cake for Ricky so we could celebrate his birthday. I kept thinking about the double rainbow. I was so excited to tell Ricky the story. I could not find a decent cake but found three yummy individual slices that worked perfectly. I bought a slice of rich deep chocolate cake, red cream velvet and a slice of German chocolate cake. When I got home, I pulled into my parking spot and noticed that the rainbows beat me home. I got out of the car and gazed at the rainbow above me as I ran up the stairs and into the house to get Ricky. When I told him that he had to see the rainbows he replied that he had already seen them. "Not these rainbows. You must see them again. These are my dad's rainbows!" Then I recounted my story of how the rainbows appeared earlier in the day. I told Ricky about my note I wrote for my Father's balloon. I just knew Ricky was created especially for me. The rainbows confirmed that I not only had God's blessing but my Father's approval too for a life-long union with Ricky.

Through color, our new outlook on life began to remove the shackles restraining us. We found the freedom to try cruise control and admire the beauty of eclectic destinations in our past, our present, and someday our future. But no matter how hard we focused on simplicity, the stubborn reality of changing and managing the carpet cleaning business continued to weigh heavily on us. The final bend in my journey with Ricky turned into a trek as if we were walking through a continuous corn maze. Sometimes living life can be like a corn maze. The life path you are on is confusing especially when your responsibilities seem overwhelming. We had interconnecting life challenges to attend to simultaneously before we could reach our final goal of sharing a perfect life together. Searching for the best approach to dealing with the business while addressing other issues in life left me feeling as if I was lost in a corn field with corn stalks towering over me. I felt as if my sense of direction was gone. Everything in life looked and felt the same. However, I believed in my heart that Ricky knew how to spiritually guide us out of the maze of the overwhelming life struggles we felt if we continued to work very hard at developing our relationship. I trusted Ricky. Ricky was very hopeful that the path ahead was clear. Hope must have come from a light because the brightness in his smile reflected light. Ricky was radiating light. Ricky took the lead and steered us through every bend and turn so that I could travel safely through each passageway. Ricky lifted me from the burdens I once carried, and he told me if we stayed together, we could reach a life far beyond our dreams.

I trusted Ricky and I believed that he could see a light that would guide our way.

"My understanding is that whatsoever is given to you is precious. If it was not so, existence would not have given it to you." ~ Osho

Mi Amor *(My Love)*

Life with Ricky was a lesson in navigating the contours of a corn maze. At times I was anxious because my life was on a path that was obscured, and I could not always see where I was destined. I felt captive in the maze, encapsulated by pillars of tall leafy stalks towering over me. Unlike the flourishing stalks, the leaves of my existence were wilting as I fretted over my future. I was overwhelmed by life and the redundancies of my daily routine. I longed to stop time so I could revisit my past and rethink pivotal decisions that would make me a different person. But Ricky encouraged me. "Hang in there!" he said. "The victory of a life together is far greater if we both try and find our way." Ricky took the lead and I graciously accepted his guidance, even when I was not sure we were on the right path. As the lessons of the maze unfolded, we carefully listened, and we followed the heart of the grain.

The corn maze was more than a road to an end. It was our life path, a deeply rooted journey with a strong thread and lifeline to my past. The corn maze was my journey through life; a journey of unexpected twists and turns. The twists could be prickly and uncomfortable. The turns could be risky and fearful. Above all, the corn maze could be the navigator's worst challenge with dark and desperate areas. I was irritated in the corn maze because I felt trapped in the density and depth of the field until Ricky guided me. He compassionately constructed lessons that taught me how to make the stalks transparent so that I could move through the maze more freely. Ricky taught me how to protect myself within the maze of life and how to protect myself from people with sharp intentions carried within their spirit. With Ricky's love as the seed carried by my heart, I learned to resist my spirit from becoming an ill sharp green blade. I sorted through feelings of being green in envy, green in ego, and green in greed and replaced them with positive feelings of renewal, calmness, and growth. Ricky taught me to peel back the pungent, russet layers of a decomposing husk so that I could release the emotions held hostage inside me. It was very liberating to learn how to release the burdens I carried. And guess what? It was that easy! Much like harvesting a crop, soil must be tilled to enable it to breathe and enhance its chemistry. When the soil is rich, life and love grow abundantly. As I pulled back a few of the prickly layers of corn husks that encased my being, I began to experience a more pleasant and tranquil life. I felt weightless and free. I felt alive! It was as if my blood had gone through dialysis and was cleansed of venomous toxins while my heart was sprinkled with a healthy shade of blush and my spirit glowed. Within nature's coat of lush green leaves lies the golden corn. Gold is symbolic of the highest power and attainment. Like the sun and golden color in corn, Ricky taught me that life and love should be golden too. Even though it felt like we were moving through life in a circle my feelings about the maze began to change. Ricky and I started walking away from a maze of dysfunction and moved forward into a life journey together. Finally, we released the need to feel anything more than just love. I was in a place where I felt truly guarded. Ricky protected me and I felt an unshakeable peace that silenced my spirit. For the first time in my life my soul was rich. Being in love is when love means everything and nothing else matters. You live to love. You love to live. Ricky taught me that pure love is not a matter of how long you love or where you are in life to love. Pure love is simply how effective the sweetness is during the time that you have it.

There is always a lesson in life to learn. The lesson unfolds as the heart opens to what the universe wants the spirit to learn. Everyone is in a corn maze at one time or another. Learning is a perpetual process. With patience and guidance, I learned the value of life. Amidst the hurried pace of my day-to-day existence, Ricky always managed to make me stop (if only for a second) so that he could create a lesson. These short pauses during our hurried day passed so quickly, like the speed of light or the blink of an eye. With each lesson, Ricky managed to create moments for me that became sparkling memories of being fully engaged in the essence of sharing our lives together. As we navigated the path in and out of each other's hearts, I felt adorned with an infinite light of love. Ricky's heart beat gloriously like a heavenly sound and the inaudible melody awoke my dormant heart so I could walk confidently out of the corn maze.

Prayer helped build my relationship with Ricky. I discovered that my inner dialog with God calmed my spirit as I prayed hard from the depth of my soul, and on bended knees. Each time I prayed I cultivated the compassion of God's love into my relationship and into my life. Love only reflects the positive. I was an integral part of the "Grand Circle of Love" where I felt the warmth gently touch my spirit repeatedly, over and over again. With prayer in my life, I felt capable of navigating any situation in life and learning from it to become a greater person. Prayer sustained my happiness and was impetus for the permanent change of my being.

Ricky captured my heart for many reasons, one of which was that he remained faithful to our love. By devoting his time to me, Ricky became a trusted friend, mentor, master and protector of my heart. Ricky professed his love for me with a vested interest in my happiness. He was able to surrender total compassion from his heart just to love me. Like nutrition for the body, my love was the single nutrient required by Ricky's soul. I learned that with love the cold feelings of darkness diminish in any circumstance. But, through the many lessons learned and prayers prayed, I believe the most important lesson for me was that love is not bound by rules or laws. Love can free anyone from a pernicious root. The common flaw and fatal error in life is the mistake of not loving yourself enough to permit yourself to be loved.

Life's difficulties have a meaning and it is not always clear how your life is being touched. Problems that once weighed so heavily on me dissipated into the blue canopy of the sky. My dwelling became the cave of Ricky's heart. Not only did I have the key to his heart, I had the key to his business accounts. Ricky gave me every account and security number for his business and his personal life. Releasing this control was monumental for Ricky and something that made me feel unconditionally trusted. Ricky also released his past to me and shared every moment of laughter from his childhood. I listened to every secret as a teenager; every sorrow, trial and tribulation he faced and felt as an adult. I even heard Ricky's untold and uncensored stories that I would have been okay not hearing. Initially, having open access to Ricky's life was like sitting in a booth behind a confession curtain. Yet I was not a priest. I was not qualified, nor did I pretend to be, to hear his life confessions. With pure love, I learned to listen compassionately. Joyfully, I pardoned Ricky from his guilt and his sins because in my spiritual eyes, Ricky was a gentle giant of God. He worked day and night and his chores never ending. He pulled his business like an ox harnessed to a heavy load and was committed to the people that worked for him. Ricky led you to believe his life was easy when it wasn't. Without hesitation, he would bear the yoke rather than give the burden to someone else. And Ricky would work even harder before giving the burden back to God. I never saw Ricky completely give up. Ricky pulled the weight of the world as if it were given to him to pull. I felt like Ricky's life and business were directly appointed to him by God and Ricky exceeded his potential 100%. Ricky gave more than his life to God. He gave God his all including his invaluable work ethic.

Ricky showed true passion in serving his clients, neighbors and employees. Over time, most became his friends and family. He desired to grow his business yet remain a humble man, which left no fortune for Ricky. He lived within humble means so that he could provide for the less fortunate. Ironically, this became his fortune. He gave opportunities to people who were down on their luck and discounts to customers for services which equated to being practically free. Ricky was the dealer of a second chance card. When he dealt you a second chance card, guaranteed he would offer a lesson on a way to a better life. Ricky was my hero because he had absolute qualities of love that could only be gifted from Heaven. That is why I loved him. There was no need for me to hear his life's confessions. Instead, I pardoned him from his personal guilt of not being more than what he could have been.

Ultimately, Ricky reached a point where he was never afraid to open up and let me inside of his heart. Ricky would say that my heart was his home and when he was home, he was able to rest. When it was time to rest Ricky talked non-stop. What I loved most about our conversations and his lessons was watching the dramatic expressions on his face as he spoke. He was so passionate. Ricky knew he captivated me when he spoke. I could not take my eyes off him. I felt compelled to listen intently to his stories, and by doing so, I learned more and more about his business.

The carpet cleaning business was born from a vision of four men. Four partners pursuing a dream and willing to do whatever it took started a business out of a trailer on a street corner the day before Christmas. They sought the American dream. The business was like a missile that launched from a rocket. It grew so quickly, it was unstoppable. However, the foundation had not settled. There were so many aspects that had to be established like payroll, telephone lines, an office supply account, and most importantly, a legal agreement with specific details about how ownership and liability would be equally split. Since there was no anticipation of failure, there was no urgency to address any of these issues during the startup of the business. Unfortunately, the four partners did not realize that most small businesses fail before they succeed. They were not prepared for the weight of sudden growth on top of a weak foundation. Over time, the financial success and impressive cash flow changed each partner's character and defined each man's greed, which led to a rift and ultimately Ricky pursuing his own business. Ricky was in business for over ten years. In one decade, a lot changed; the location of his office, the number of employees, and the competition. The longevity of having his own business had an adverse impact on Ricky's personal life because he was chained to the business and worked hard, physically and emotionally to make it work. The business was not always bad for Ricky. Materially speaking, it gave Ricky a very good life. But the past mistakes from his business partnerships haunted him and denied him from reaching his dream. Ricky wanted a corporate jet. He wanted to feel the power of the engines beneath his feet. He wanted to soar.

Ricky shared his stories about different carpet cleaning jobs. I could tell that inside his heart Ricky loved being in the lives of his clients. Some of Ricky's more regular clients became his very dear friends. I even learned to consider some of them to be like my own "family." Ricky's client stories were so diverse, ranging from the most common to the extreme in the categories of culture, wealth, demographics and even cleanliness.

Ricky had clients who were in the military. Colorado Springs, Colorado where Ricky's business was established is home to the U.S. Air Force Academy, so the area is populated with current and former military personnel. Typically, the military clients' homes were adorned with service ribbons, awards and honors positioned like trophies throughout the house. High ranking Colonels proudly decorated their hallways with prestigious medals for their service and contribution to their country. Many of the retired servicemen encouraged Ricky to change his career. Ricky would jokingly boast about his business and tell them, "You can't just trust anybody in your home. I offer home land security!" But Ricky did take note of the advice he was given about changing his career, especially as he got older. Undeniably, Ricky's body was aging and even though he appeared physically fit, Ricky had persistent aches and pains throughout his body. Even with the advice he was given, I could tell Ricky struggled with that one question, "Where do I start when this is all that I know?" In addition, Ricky felt that if he left the business, he would be abandoning his employees. The military clients shared more than advice. They took advantage of Ricky's presence to share war stories and stories of lost love.

Ricky heard one story about a long-distance love that flourished into many years when two people were reunited after being separated because of a call to serve in active duty. Ricky shared his story about how he joined the Air Force when he was a teenager but was released due to an allergic reaction to the vaccinations. As Ricky talked about his conversations with the military clients, I know he tossed a thought around in his mind. It was the same thought I had. What would have my life been like if Ricky were able to serve his country? I also wondered if Ricky's life path was different, would I have still been a part of his life and a part of him?

Although Ricky did not serve in the U.S. Air Force, he still offered a public service through a sincere and heartfelt obligation to his elderly women clients. I refer to these Grandmotherly clients as "Mama Grandes" or matriarchs of the family. Like the service men, Mama Grandes had photos too. Family photos were everywhere in their homes. There were photos placed on top of photos, curled slightly and yellow with age, photos hanging in frames that did not always fit the frame, and photos standing upright in the middle of delicately crocheted doilies that had so much starch they were stiff as boards. Ricky told me that every Mama Grande's home had a table near the front door right by the stairway. The "honorary table" was a place setting of the soul and contained an altar and trinkets that could reveal an entire life story. Anything and everything were selected for display on the altar, such as a personal collection of colorful rocks which were always hand selected and carefully arranged in the shape of a heart, or a statue of a Saint draped with long strings of plastic rosary beads. Ricky told me that once he even saw a set of teeth soaking in a clear glass jar. I explained that these Mothers used their tables as safe harbors (lack of a better term) for their sentimental stuff collected over the years. Because nothing went to waste, they also used their tables for personal items like long black hairpins, eyeglasses, and even the false teeth that made their smiles complete. Above all, these women produced offspring, who in turn produced offspring, who produced offspring. A big family was a blessed family but not necessarily a cooperative one. Ricky told me that he could never effectively clean the Mama Grandes' carpet because her family was always present, walking in and out of rooms and running up and down the stairs, turning the home into more of a Grand Central Station than a domicile in a quiet neighborhood. Despite this, Ricky was devoted to his Mama Grande clients and they loved their carpet cleaning man who gave them "the family" discount.

Equally as important as the Mama Grandes, another group of clients that received special treatment from Ricky were the "Viejitas" (old women). Unlike the Mama Grandes that had tons of family circling amongst them, the Viejitas lived alone. They lived in the poverty of being outcasts of society because of their age and their looks. Ricky described the Viejitas' homes as showing no signs of love or being loved. These women were not cared for and even worse, some were left alone and forgotten, essentially abandoned. Ricky hurt to see the Viejitas like this. So, in addition to cleaning their carpets, Ricky offered the Viejitas "face lifts." When they heard his earnest greeting, "Hello Sweetie!" the Viejitas basked in the attention and reacted with an enthusiastic smile. I know how they felt. I always broke out in a smile every time Ricky greeted me with these two feel-good words. Ricky loved to see his Viejitas smile because he said it brought back their youthful beauty, if only for a moment. "If my Viejitas could only see their beauty from within, they would own a gallery of beautiful photos to display for each and every day of their entire life." Miraculously, these elderly women lived on a very tight budget but always found a way to have their carpets cleaned. Perhaps it was their investment in the best medication they could take because a day with Ricky was a day that they could smile and feel good. It was also a day they could give back. Smiling was contagious and Ricky would catch the symptoms and smile back at them, especially when he discovered the cookies in their oven were made just for him. Cookies were only a few of the rewards bestowed upon Ricky by the Viejitas. Ricky also received other baked goods and handmade crochet items, and he loved them all. Sometimes Ricky's workday was extended because of the time he spent listening to the Viejitas' stories. The Viejitas always managed to negotiate a few extra services from Ricky like throwing out their trash and changing light bulbs that had burned out months ago. Ricky always cared that his Viejitas had at least one working light on inside their home because it could very well be the only light shining in their life. Ricky never had a problem helping his Viejitas. In a sense, they reminded him of his Mother. His Mother also lived alone. Ricky felt that if his Mother was in a similar situation, he would want someone to be kind to her and help her out regardless.

The pages of Ricky's life were filled with so many notable on-the-job stories. Some stories tugged at the heartstrings while others were not worth repeating. There was one particular job Ricky talked about that was very different from the other jobs. The story moved me so much. What happened may have had a spiritual impact on our life path. I call this story, "*Un Día Con Dios*" or a Day with God. What made this job so special was how Ricky told the story and the fact that this was the last job story Ricky shared with me.

I vividly remember that morning because of the mackerel clouds. They rippled against the ominous sky like the dark silver scales of a fish traversing downstream. The clouds brought rain showers from the east that quickly turned into thunderstorms, a surreptitious sign of instability. It was the day after payday. Ricky was sitting at the edge of the couch listening to his voice mail. His morning crew had already called in sick. The messages were left in the middle of the night while Ricky's cell phone was turned off. Ricky had nothing to look forward to that morning and the weight of the world started to descend upon his shoulders. The glowing embers of the sun did not illuminate for him that day. In the absence of light, the feeling of doom was inescapable for both of us. Life was no longer golden but a dark shade of grey. Ricky sat expressionless on the couch as if he were looking behind the iron bars of a cold jail cell. His facial expression displayed the inherent depression from another day of working alone. I had to act quickly. I knew I had to be his light, so I started singing cheerful good morning songs in the shower. When Ricky knocked on the bathroom door, I opened it just enough so that he could peak in at me. Droplets of water were sprayed all over my face. They were like tiny electrical bursts of energy coming from my eyes, mouth and cheeks. Before Ricky could give me his bad news, I interrupted him and said, "Today is going to be the best day ever, I can feel it!" Ricky's head was already hanging low. He reached forward to kiss me goodbye tasting the sparkles of water on my lips. I told him that he was the best husband in the world. As Ricky started to pick his head up, I placed my hand under his chin and raise his head even higher and gave him his blessing for a safe return home. He smiled at me and then stepped out into a day of work that he could never have anticipated.

Ricky arrived at his office and opened the front door to witness one of his employees diligently working in the telephone room. Her name was Lucy or "Luz" for short which in Spanish means "light." Lucy was in her late fifties and looked like she had indulged in one too many Thanksgiving dinners. She was fluent in Spanish and spoke with a heavy accent. Lucy would often greet Ricky in the morning with a robust, "Buenos Días Señor Guapo," (Good morning Mr. Handsome). That morning Lucy informed Ricky that every employee had called the office to say they would not be coming in today. When she saw how upset Ricky became, she wisely changed the subject and told Ricky that she received a call from a church that wanted a room cleaned for "mucho dinero" (a lot of money)! The church would only schedule the work if they were assured that the job would be completed that day. Without a staff to delegate the work, Ricky grabbed the job ticket, loaded his equipment in the truck, and ventured out to do the job alone. Working solo would give Ricky the opportunity to think. He needed to mentally sort through the necessary changes that he had to make in the office. The day grew a little brighter for Ricky. Being in a house of prayer would give Ricky a chance to personally deliver his prayer request to the church altar. But Ricky's story turned to frustration when he told me that Lucy did not know the difference between a room in a church and an entire Synagogue! Although the job offered "mucho dinero," it was a tenth of his regular rate for an area that size.

Staring at the Synagogue from his truck Ricky decided that he did not want to turn down the job. He hopped out of his truck and was approached by someone from the Church who was waiting patiently for him to arrive. Ricky politely explained that his employee who took the call quoted the wrong price. Ricky being Ricky, I was not surprised when he told me that instead of getting a fair rate for the job already quoted, he decided he would clean the main sanctuary, the adjacent social hall, and the offices at slightly half of his regular rate. The Synagogue got a much better deal with Ricky offering to clean an even larger area. Naturally, the Synagogue quickly accepted. I do not know if it was Ricky's stubborn determination, his heart of gold, or his mind over matter that made Ricky think he could handle a job that size all by himself. But that is what he thought. I could picture Ricky pleading with God for a little extra help as he approached his truck to gather his supplies without a second thought about what he had just negotiated. Ready to face the day's project, Ricky stared curiously through the front doors of the Synagogue. He felt a bit self-conscious about his mission to deliver his prayer request. His desperate need to ask for good workers made his entry through the front doors a little easier. Before he stepped into the Synagogue, he took a deep breath and released the morning tension that was trapped in every muscle of his body. Ricky did not want to disturb anyone in the Synagogue, so he quietly arranged his equipment in one corner then started working. Being in a house of prayer was a relief for Ricky. He spoke of the experience as if he were given a special time in a sacred place. Even though Ricky did not wear the traditional "Yarmulke", he respected the Synagogue and what it represented. It was being in this place that Ricky felt a spiritual connection far beyond the bricks and mortar of the Synagogue's highest point. And every time that Ricky put his work-beaten hands on the floor to pick up a few specks of dirt he prayed.

Ricky prayed as he worked. He prayed in his own unique way. He prayed the way he was taught while serving as an Altar Boy in a small-town Catholic Church. In the Synagogue Ricky wept silently in God's ear, and God helped Ricky peel back the many layers of bitterness coating his soul; bitterness Ricky had for so many people, including his employees, who had taken from him and lied to him. As Ricky cleansed the carpet of the dirt deposited deep into the fabric, he cleansed himself and released the toxic bitterness that plagued him so deeply for so many years. The job that was to bring Ricky "mucho dinero" gave him so much more instead. It turned into a journey of receiving total forgiveness lifting his heart from bondage. That day Ricky found an eternal light in the Synagogue that brought him hope and a new direction.

There is a reason for everything. There was a reason the Synagogue called that day. The memory of how Ricky walked out of the room after telling me the story of *Un Día Con Dios* is evidence of this. Ricky was different. He was larger than life. I could see every tendon flex in his body; with each step Ricky took I felt his power. He walked with confidence in his stride and proudly held his head high. His shoulders were no longer weighed down with worry. He was truly lifted from his burdens and appeared almost luminous. Looking at Ricky made me realize that he and I were never lost in our life journey, even when we were in a maze of life and did not know what direction to take. We managed to move forward through every obstacle knowing that we had each other. Most of all, we called upon a much higher light to guide us through the treacherous twists and turns. Ricky's motive was love. I remember feeling trapped in the corn maze. Before I met Ricky, my spirit was longing to be loved. Ricky saw this. With his love, Ricky conveyed to me his lessons that gave my spirit a glowing balance of harmony and peace. Shortly after I heard the story of "*Un Día Con Dios*," I reached a higher level in my personal life knowing there were many blessings within our reach. Despite this, I was still not prepared for what was about to happen to me.

The night was clear and uneventful. I plodded through the evening shadows on my drive home, pausing at a red traffic light that seemed to catch me at every corner. It was as if the traffic lights had faulty problems of their own. While stopped at a red traffic light I remembered hearing a siren. I looked around but could not determine from which direction the sound came. My soul was racing home ahead of me. I kept thinking about Ricky and our plans. I was talking to Ricky in my mind as I was driving, telling him we must move faster. We must close the Colorado Springs office and move it to Denver. We must cut spending. We must hire a different crew. We must sit down and finalize the wedding plans. We must start living one life together. When I finally arrived at home, I pulled into a corner parking space. I slowly got out of the car and opened the back door to grab a bag of groceries. I closed the back door and I started walking up the steps to the apartment. It was summer, it was hot, and I was exhausted.

When I approached the front door, I heard the television. Through the closed door I could hear that Ricky was watching another of his entertaining wrestling matches. I could hear the crowd screaming in jubilation and triumph over the winner's victory. With the key in my right hand I inserted it into the lock and turned it slightly. Instantly, the door swung open. The door stayed wide open. Initially, I thought Ricky had opened the door because he always opened the door for me. I looked to the right of the door where he usually stood, but he was not there. Then I looked straight ahead. Ricky was collapsing right in front of me. Something was terribly wrong!

Ricky is kneeling on his left knee, his right knee bent forward but his leg is almost twisted beneath him. His head is down, his chin almost digging into his chest. His right arm is reaching up to the ceiling as if to grab someone's hand. His left hand is in a tight fist in line with his left hip. He was holding on. I let the bag of groceries slip out of my left hand. I rush over and grab the telephone from its cradle on the floor. As I am holding the phone in my right hand, I am dialing 9-1-1. I fall to my knees and quickly lift Ricky into my arms. I see his eyes come into contact with mine. His eyes focus on my face but then I notice that his eyes start to roll back with his breath. I start kissing him on his forehead. I tell him, "I'm home, I'm home... everything will be fine." He rests his head on my chest. Frantically, I look around the room, yelling for someone to help me. I look straight ahead. The front door is still wide open. There is food on a coffee table. What is happening? Within seconds after I call 9-1-1 the line rings and someone picks up. A 911 operator is now walking me through the process of how to save Ricky's life. I now have help. Someone on the telephone is helping me. The male voice on the other side tells me I must do exactly as I am instructed. I am now being told how to try and keep Ricky alive. I am instructed to lay Ricky flat on the floor. Immediately, I try to lift him up toward me. I am able to create a space where I can lay Ricky down flat on his back. I anxiously ask the male voice on the other end, "What do I do now?" I am listening to every detail... every word. The room is cold. The breeze from the air conditioner helps me stay focused. I am breathing for both of us.

Ricky's heart abruptly stopped pumping blood; he is having a cardiac arrest. His heart muscle is dying from lack of oxygen. A sudden cardiac arrest is very serious and is life threatening. I only have a few minutes to help him. Ricky is showing no signs of response when I call out to him. He is collapsing into an unconscious state. I am kneeling above him close to his left side. As instructed, I place my fingers into his mouth to clear out any food. I had to scoop out whatever he was eating but there was no food in his mouth. Then, I am instructed to place my hands firmly one on top of the other near the center of his chest. I am told to press down quickly while counting "One," lift up and then press down again and count, "Two." I am giving Ricky chest compressions which will move the blood from his heart and into his brain. My voice echoes in and out of my mind as I count. I try hard to release the fog and regain total focus. My breathing gets heavy with every inhale and deeper with every exhale. My eyes are exhausted as I try to find signs of life in the moment. My eyes suddenly fill with tears. But before my tears can fall, I look up at the ceiling, for faith... help? I am calling on higher powers. I am calling for God. I am praying hard. I did not want Ricky to see my face. I did not want him to feel my tears. My face and my tears will show Ricky that his condition is life threatening. I held on firmly. I sink my teeth into my bottom lip, and then I continue counting while trying not to cry as I look down at him.

"One, two...one, two...one, two..." each number is precisely pronounced one second apart. I feel the hardness of the floor through the layer of the carpet. The floor feels extremely hard on my bended knees as I pressed both of my hands down on Ricky's chest. The floor helped ground me so that I can press down. My body is heavy. I am warm from the extreme heat of the summer. "One, two...one, two...one, two...one, two..." I plead, "Come on, STAY with me!" My voice is now echoing in desperation. I can barely say the word, "Wa-ah-nnn." I keep pushing my knees harder and harder against the floor. I am determined to save him! I release the word, "Ta-woo." My hands are still one on top of the other as I am pressing down quickly; "One two, one two." I scream "God, please help me!... One, two...one, two..." the words are getting longer to pronounce as I am saying them, "Wa---uhn.....t-ooh..." A soft voice inside tells me to breathe. In my heart I am having a conversation with Ricky, "Please baby, please hold on... We're getting married!" Inside my mind I keep giving my own instructions to stay focused, you got this.... YOU GOT THIS! He is going to make it! Out loud I am telling Ricky, "Stay with me! Please, please baby, please stay with me!" "I GOT THIS!"

"One, two...one, two...one, two..." my head is tilted so that my left shoulder can hold the telephone close to my ear. On the other end the 911 operator is talking, "You're doing fine, keep counting. I want to hear you count!" In the background, I hear footsteps running up the stairs. Finally, there is some reassurance! I hear a whisper. "They're coming, hang in there baby!" The footsteps grow louder and closer. The footsteps are pounding now. I tell the 911 operator "Someone is running up the stairs, I can hear them!" The 911 operator tells me "Keep counting, let me hear you. You're doing fine!" "One, two.... one, two... one, two..." the counting is getting easier and faster because I know help is near. "One, two.... one, two... one, two..." I look up but still no one is there. Ricky and I are still alone together in the room. With one hand on top of the other trying helplessly to maintain a heartbeat I am desperately gasping for air when I realized I am breathing in his last breath. I am by his side trying desperately to save him. "WHERE ARE THEY?" I scream out loud, "HELP ME!" I hear a loud voice burst into the room "We're here!" I look up and I see four or five paramedics spill through the open doorway. They quickly pull a glass table away to clear the area. They drop their medical supplies on the floor. I see the opened clear plastic medical supply packages on the ground. A breathing tube is placed in Ricky's mouth. I hear the word, "Clear!" I hear a thump. I hear short beeps. I am sitting in the corner on the floor. I cannot stand up. I push myself backwards with my knees bent. Helplessly, I start dragging my body off to the side of the room. I am trying hard to get out of the way. I become separated from Ricky. I can no longer feel him. I lose it and all my emotions are evident on my face. I start crying. I cannot stop the tears from falling. I am falling. I lost Ricky's touch and Ricky lost mine.

I curl my knees to my chest and wrap my arms around my legs. I start rocking my body into the cold wall. Once again, I try to regain focus. It is like I am floating away after Ricky. I feel my wings, but I cannot fly. I keep thinking I must help him! I must believe that Ricky will be okay. I need a Bible! Somehow, I manage to get up and I can stand on my own. I run into the bedroom, open a dresser drawer, and grab Ricky's Bible. I run back into the room and sit down on the floor. I run my fingers down the middle spine of the Bible. I open the Bible and start praying. I ask God for a message to comfort me. When I start reading the Bible, I hear someone say, "We are not getting a heartbeat!" As I slowly raise my head, the weight of my heart painfully knocks my head back down. My eyes land on the words in a page of the Bible. As I am reading the Bible, I discard the words I just heard. I am reaching out for "hope." My spirit is comforted with the Bible, so I keep reading. I cling to the Bible as if it is my lifeline. I see a scripture. In silence, I am reading the following Bible passage from my heart, "the righteous cry out, and the Lord hears them; He delivers them from all their troubles," Psalm 34:17. I know Ricky is gone. God heard Ricky's cry and He delivered him from his pain. Ricky is dead and I am in shock sitting still and lost in a moment of time. Someone comes over to me and sits directly in front of me. With a pale look on my face and a nauseated feeling in my stomach, I listen to the words, "I am so sorry for your loss." The room is now silent. I can no longer hear what is being said. I fade out from the room completely as my spirit is gone too.

I often relive July 18, 2011, the night Ricky died. As I think about it, I always seem to be somewhere off in the distance. The moment does not seem real. I remember being still and lost in my own feelings. I think about what more I could have done. Did I do it right? I also think about what I did correctly. It all happened so suddenly; in such a brief snapshot of time I was losing my love. I must remember that night so that I do not forget. If I forget, I am afraid that I will leave life with Ricky behind.

I am convinced the night Ricky died was an event carefully orchestrated by God. Each second was a critical moment in the final stages of Ricky's life here on this earth. I know that time was on our side, and everything happened according to His greater plan. If I had arrived one second earlier, I could have heard Ricky's painful cries for help. But I did not. Hearing Ricky cry out for help would have destroyed me. If I had arrived one second later, I could have found Ricky lying on top of the glass table. But he did not. He could have crashed into the glass table and died before I got there. But he did not. The precise moment that Ricky's soul left this world was masterfully timed. I found Ricky at the exact moment that I was supposed to find him. He was kneeling with one knee bent. His head resting upon his chest and his right hand raised toward the ceiling as if God was saying, "Well done my child. You are home." I believe the night when Ricky died, when I walked up three flights of stairs and put my key in the front door, something was there. Something, was on the other side of the door, the door opened for me. I was NEVER able to open the door with my key and get in so quickly. I had to wiggle the key in the lock and turn the knob so many times to the left and right. Because it was hard to unlock the door, I had even accused Ricky of changing the locks. I believe that Divine intervention opened the door that night, at the precise moment of

Ricky's passing. Ricky fought to hold on and wait for me to come home so that he could go "home". Ricky knew how important it was for him to have his best friend by his side. His Grandfather always told him, "When you die if you have only one person by your side then you did really good in life."

Things happen for a reason. I had to experience this miraculous yet devastating event. I was back in the corn maze called life holding Ricky as he lay dying in my arms. There was no way out but up. As heartbreaking as it was for me, I believe through Ricky's death there is something greater being gifted to my life. Because Ricky died in grace and dignity my soul tried to go with him. I was holding on to Ricky but his soul left me. As my soul drifted after him, I was able to watch him go as far as I could go. I was left standing by the sea on a bridge gazing out at the curls of the ocean waves. In each bend, the water moved with the breath of the wind, back and forth, up and down, side to side, and as the waves continued to proceed outward the water lifted Ricky further and further away from me. That is when I felt what Heaven must be like.

With the final beat of Ricky's heart, I caught a glimpse of Heaven. I traveled beyond the boundaries of time as if I drifted from the reality of that room to the serenity of Heaven. I felt Heaven's existence far beyond the awe-inspiring great blue sky. I smelled an amazing aroma of Heaven's sweet floral gardens. The blossoms of peace lingered in the air all around me as if I was the beneficiary bouquet of the gardens. Love was abundant. Love changed me and all I could do was smile and be happy knowing that Ricky was home. When Ricky's heart stopped beating, his life journey ended and my life journey was about to begin. Feeling the powerful presence of love from Heaven taught me that I must love myself before I can be loved. When I lost Ricky, I realized the reverse is just as relevant. The love I was given continues to live within my heart. I had to retain love, or I would be lost.

Ricky left an imprint of love inside my heart, and with his imprint, I had to find my own way.

> "Love is just a word until you find someone to give it a definition."
> ~ Unknown

Te Quiero (I Love You)

Divine love is a gift. Ricky taught me this through his compassion and benevolence for me. He believed in me and gave me the passcode to his soul. His signature is engraved in the center of my heart, and I wear it with dignity and honor. Some people spend years searching yet never catch a glimpse of the love Ricky and I had experienced over time. Our love was truly a gift.

It was the night before Ricky died, a night just like any other. I was sleeping comfortably when Ricky woke me up because he felt the light of the moon reach out to him through the crack in the Venetian blind and extend a lingering touch on the side of his face. Ricky sat up in bed and asked me, "Why did you let the moon into our room?" Then, he got out of bed and walked toward the beam of frosty pink light shimmering through our bedroom window. He did not stop at the window but went outside and stood on the deck. I had no idea what he was talking about when he referenced the moon, but it was intentional. I often wonder what he was thinking while he stood on the deck looking up at her majesty. Was there a secret code in the moon's appearance to Ricky? Did the moon bring Ricky a promise of something yet to come? Did she whisper assurance to Ricky that she would be the lighthouse to guide him on his final journey over the ocean as he traveled safely home? Or was the moon meant for me? Did she want me to know that she would be the light in my life during my darkest hours? What was this powerful premonition from the moon?

After I lost Ricky, I began to feel a spiritual connection to the moon. I was curious to understand what purpose the moon served that Sunday evening the seventeenth of July 2011. I was surprised when I discovered so many moon names with various meanings. The moon phase that night was a Waning Gibbous Moon and it follows a Full Moon Phase becoming less luminated night by night. This Moon phase signifies gratitude a quality of being thankful. There are basic facts about the moon like how it orbits our planet and contributes to the ocean tides on Earth. There are also spiritual facts about the moon. I needed to know why that moon appeared in our bedroom window that night as if it were dispatched specifically for Ricky. I needed to comprehend the inherent wisdom of the moon's speechless message. A precious gift that came out of my research of the moon was that I allowed myself to believe in what I felt. I freed myself from the wonder or worry about what others would think of me if I dared to believe differently so I opened my heart and I was seeing, hearing and feeling through the crimson center of my being.

I believe the moon is a pearl of wisdom, a funnel of light that enabled Ricky to have an intuitive sense of the event that was scheduled to change our lives in the next twenty-four hours. The moon was a calculator of time; a timepiece with each precious second ticking away, beat by beat. The moon was a teacher with a lesson in yin yang that I had to learn. The moon in its platinum metal is the complementary opposite of the sun in its glittering gold. The universe is the dynamic system that brings moon and sun together. Ricky became like the moon, shining his radiant silvery light on me, encouraging me to shine like glittering gold in my life. With a spiritual focus on the moon, I felt warm again instead of being cold. I may never know the true reason for the moon making its appearance on that pivotal night, but I know it was not just any moon. Ricky wanted me to know that I let the moon into our bedroom. I let the moon into our lives. I concluded that although many people study the moon, they never actually stepped foot on the moon and there is still much more we must learn about her mysteries.

My heightened spirituality began with the moon but expanded into other aspects of my life. Once again, my life became embellished with color. This time, I received a gift of seven colors: red, orange, yellow, green, blue, indigo, and violet; specially packaged, in a handwoven spectacular arch against the sky, a rainbow! Unlike my Father's rainbows, when I saw this rainbow, I felt the light and rays of color from Ricky's love. My heart leapt silently. Irish legends describe leprechauns holding black pots filled with gold found at the end of every rainbow. The scientific explanation of a rainbow is an optical phenomenon that occurs when white light is refracted into its spectrum of colors. The Biblical explanation of a rainbow is God's promise of love and a covenant for all life on earth. It was the rainbow that embraced me with God's love after Ricky died. When I opened my heart to the rainbow, I witnessed its physical and metaphysical beauty and rainbows began appearing everywhere. It was as if the rainbow was moving independently, a life-form, like a human being traveling with me and never wanting to leave my side. The rainbow was no longer materialized in the sky above me but appeared in my hand! It happened at work one day. I left the office to get lunch. I ordered my lunch "to go" so I could eat at my desk; the office was quiet, so I was hoping to get a lot done. The to-go container was black styrofoam with a clear plastic lid. Inside I had golden onion rings and a hardy hot Reuben sandwich. I was missing Ricky so much that day. I had a five-minute walk back to work and I thought about him. I walked with my head down and my heart heavy. A few tears fell from my eyes and landed on the plastic lid of the food container like raindrops against a windshield. I was about to use my sleeve to wipe the tears off when I saw a hologram of a rainbow on the plastic lid. I quickly looked up to the sky and thanked God for the reminder that I was loved. When I got back to the office, I proudly displayed my rainbow and let my food get cold in the container, refusing to disturb the tears on the plastic lid that like rain from the sky, brought the rainbow to me.

Precious gifts and special messages of love are not only found in rainbows, objects or in signs, but can be exchanged by warm and genuine gestures.

I felt the extension of love from family and close friends with whom I had established a personal relationship. I also felt love from many people that stepped into my life just to let me know that I was in their prayers. The most treasured acknowledgement was from a male clerk working in a grocery store. He was in the parking lot tediously pushing the grocery carts toward the entrance of the store. When the clerk crossed my path, he looked directly up at me and offered a simple smile. His teeth were not perfect. Yet, his smile was so much brighter than people with perfect teeth that it stretched across and illuminated the parking lot. This smile gave me hope that I could complete the simple task of buying food so I could eat again. His smile made me return to the same store on three different occasions. I wanted to know if he was an angel. Every time I saw him, he was smiling at the entire world in front of him. It was as if he saw past pain, anger, anguished eyes and sadness. He was happy; happy to be alive and offer his smile to the world. There are many people in the world that do not or cannot extend the gesture freely. I had yet to master the art of gifting my smile back to the world. I had to learn to smile again. For the time being, I decided to leave this task to the special angels; angels that find you in everyday places if you open your heart to see them.

I never had patience for dealing with negative people. Instead, I preferred a positive perspective, a perspective of light and not darkness. A week before Ricky died, I had an appointment to talk to a counselor about releasing all negative people from my work and personal life. I had been struggling at work with some negativity that was toxic to my health, my spirit, and overall being. I ached to free myself from the grasp of a very disturbing and difficult force. I scheduled an appointment with a counselor named Lesly. Initially, I wanted an appointment with a spiritual, holistic healer by the name of Christy, but tried three weeks earlier with no luck. I was desperate for professional help because the two years I invested in saying and reading daily affirmations were no longer working for me. When searching for a counselor with empathy and compassion, I was referred to two male and two female counselors, but no one returned my call except Lesly. Her voice was very pleasant over the telephone, so I scheduled an appointment with her without hesitation.

I arrived ten minutes early at my appointment to make sure I was at the correct location. I stood in front of a closed door reading the numbers on the wall. I read the name of the office. I was confused. Then the most ironic thing happened. I was standing at the office for Christy, who was the holistic healer. "Who is Lesly? Was Lesly with the holistic healer's office or was she returning my call for counseling? Am I with the counselor or am I with the holistic healer?" When Lesly opened the door, I saw a massage table which added to my confusion. I was not sure what to expect but I was a willing patient open to receiving any form of treatment. Lesly asked me to sit in a chair across from her. Admittedly, I wanted to jump up on the massage table and be healed spiritually. I imagine I gave Lesly the impression that I was a complete looney as I nervously looked around the room exhibiting signs of panic, possibly a manic, maybe even depressed. Yet, I felt like I should be there. It felt right. This office, this place, this room, it was all very familiar to me. Oddly, I was not thinking this to myself; I was actually talking out loud. "I am supposed to be here, this is very weird. I'm so confused!" My actions finally made sense to Lesly when I stopped to explain that I was trying to contact Christy, and I was also seeking a counselor. What still did not make sense to me was how I met Lesly when I never had her name or number. Lesly looked at my list of counselors. She recognized one of the telephone numbers and told me that she shared the same phone number with one of the male counselors that was on my "I must call now" list. That is why she returned my call. We both agreed that the story was extremely coincidental, but Lesly reassured me that it was probably meant for me to be there. I finally felt some relief from the tension and confusion I was feeling.

During my first visit Lesly noticed how connected I was with my own feelings as well as the feelings of others. She told me that I was hooked to a few negative people, and together, we would determine how to get the negative feelings unhooked from me. I referred to Lesly as my personal advisor. I loved that I was able to talk openly to her. Lesly told me I was not a wall flower. She encouraged me to believe that I was important, and I had to get down from the wall and make a difference. My first office visit was wonderful. I scheduled an appointment with Lesly the following week. That evening Christy's husband called me. I was able to schedule time with Christy two hours before my next appointment with Lesly. I was being reeled in by that office. My mind, body and spirit were open to receiving more information in order to move beyond the negative feelings that had crashed into me.

My scheduled appointment with both Christy and Leslie was three days after Ricky passed away. I was hurting profusely, wounded from head to toe and in need of a body size Band-Aid. I must have written down the date of the appointment incorrectly because I waited for Christy, but she never arrived. I was lying on a bench outside of her office in a long hallway. The building was old with creaky floors and cold walls. I felt very uncomfortable in the hallway and was being watched by other people walking in and out of their offices. I decided to leave and come back later for my appointment with Lesly. When I reached into my pocket to grab my car keys, I remembered that my sister drove me to the appointment because she was worried that I would not able to focus behind a steering wheel. I jumped into the elevator and walked out of the front door into a bright summer day. It had cooled down enough to appreciate the warmth of the summer. The temperature was perfect for an afternoon stroll. When I started my walk, Ricky quickly came to mind; maybe he had never left my mind. With my left arm down at my side, I allowed my fingers to open up as if my hand slipped into Ricky's hand and then I curled my fingers shut. I imagined that he was walking next to me.

I heard Ricky say, "Sweetie, look at the flowers."

But I did not want to look at the flowers. Instead, I looked down at the ground and focused on the cracks in the sidewalk. I started to jump over the cracks like a little girl playing hopscotch.

In a little girl's voice, I playfully told Ricky, "If I stepped on a crack, I would break my mama's back."

Ricky must have had professional street pavers with him because the cracks in the sidewalk mysteriously faded one by one until they were all gone. With my head still hanging low, I inhaled one deep breath and smelled an overpowering fragrance in the nearby gardens. Then, I looked to the right and as I exhaled, I noticed the amazing beauty of the summer flowers in full bloom to which Ricky referred too. The vibrant colors of the overlapping petals were exceptionally striking, and the leaves were more gorgeous then ever in various bright shades of green. Ricky did not mention the butterflies hovering over the marigold flowers with their frail wings fluttering, the bees buzzing steadily in and out of the core of each gladiolus, or the lovely lady bugs balancing on the blossoms. I suppose that was something solely for me to see.

The conversation instinctively began as I imagined Ricky was with me. I started talking aloud.

> I said, "Baby, do you remember our walk after your birthday? You made sure that I walked on the inside of the street. We were just like couples in the olden days when they had proper manners and etiquette."
>
> Ricky said, "Yes, I remember."
>
> I continued speaking, "I remember too, we walked so far it felt like we were walking down every street in Colorado. Do you remember me pointing at everything around us?"
>
> Ricky said, "Yes, I remember."

I wanted to know about the boy's correctional facility and the apartment complexes surrounding the facility. It rained the week before and I wanted to know why the water drains had backed up. There were puddles of water everywhere and water was running off and into the street.

I asked Ricky, "What is the safest road I can take that would lead me back home?"

Ricky said, "Stay off of the busy streets because of the heavy traffic and stay off the side streets that had a dim light."

It was Ricky's final decision that I should always stay with him so he can safely guide me home. On our walk, Ricky showed me two different trees that were growing old together. The trees were a good distance apart, but nature turned one of the trees up and out of the ground. It looked like one of the tree branches lay lowered as if it sacrificed its life in order to feel the personal touch from the other tree. The branch was like a plank offering the other tree the foundation and support it needed to survive.

I said, "Do you remember when I climbed the two trees? Then I got stuck and you had to help me down."

Ricky said, "Yes, I remember. I wanted to take a break so I could admire the stars that were shining in your eyes."

I said, "You stood up and shouted, I am the luckiest husband this world could ever have!"

We were both so happy. We were shedding tears of joy! I remember telling Ricky about how he had me on a pedestal and how I cut the legs off so if I fell off the pedestal, I would not hurt myself.

Ricky said, "I fixed your pedestal when you were sleeping. I designed the highest pedestal anyone woman could ever sit on. Don't worry. You will always be safe. I will see to that. I give you my word. You will never, fall or get hurt again. I will be watching over you forever."

For an hour, I strolled around the neighborhood feeling as if Ricky was with me. I was enjoying the conversation when I realized that I had to walk back to meet with Lesly. I got back just in the nick of time. Lesly was holding the office door open for me. I placed my things on the chair by the door and I sat down across from her. The first thing she said was, "What's wrong?" I told her that Ricky died in my arms. I was trying to spiritually heal quickly so I did not have to feel the pain in my heart. Lesly shook her head as if she were screaming to me, "NO, NO, NO!" Lesly told me, "That is not how it is done." She suggested that I allow myself to feel whatever it was I had to feel. My first thought was that I could emerge myself in water. In a compassionate voice Leslie told me to take life easy while I allow myself time to heal. I was instructed to do whatever I needed to do in order to feel better. Lesly escorted me out of her office and told me that when I was ready to see her again to give her a call and schedule an appointment. She sat with me outside of the building until my sister arrived. Then, Lesly said that she believed in spirits. She said they hang around for a few days to say their final goodbyes. She told me it was okay for me to open my heart and feel Ricky as if he were right next to me. I did not get my body size Band-Aid that day. I received something much better; I received "hope." I had hope that I could still talk to Ricky. Hope, that maybe, just maybe, Ricky still might be listening.

When I got home, I prepared a hot bath with very fragrant bubbles. While the water filled up in the tub, I checked my phone for messages. Earlier in the day, I received a voice message from Ricky's sister. She was with Ricky's Mother back in Florence making the funeral arrangements. They asked me to send a photo of Ricky for the memorial that would be printed in the newspaper. Naturally, the Internet was slow to load as I searched for the right photo. In the interim, I placed one of Ricky's photos as the wallpaper on my computer screen. I did not want my bathwater to turn cold so I thought I would enjoy my bath first, then send the photo. I jumped into the inviting tub and felt the bubbles tickle my body. The water was brown from a packet of herbal mud I tossed into the tub. I was so relaxed.

My heart was finally at peace. As I submerged myself in the healing water with my eyes closed, I concentrated on my breaths, allowing my tummy to expand out and contract back in with each inhalation of my breath. I laid back with my head against the edge of the tub and let the warm water hold me and caress my body. My eyes were still closed when I resumed the conversation I had earlier in the day when I was walking with Ricky.

> I said, "Ricky I don't know what happened. Everything is happening so quickly. I am not taking the time to take care of the things in my own life. I cannot pick myself up and continue taking care of things for you. I can't do it. I need you!"

I was scolding myself for not being with his Mother while she made the funeral arrangements. I asked Ricky to please step in and help his Mother with his arrangements.

> I asked Ricky, "Please, help us with your final resting place. Where do you want to be buried?"

> I begged him, "Ricky please; please try hard to make the arrangements fall into place because your Mother was in shock and she is grieving too."

> As I cried, I told Ricky, "I am so sorry for everything that I did not do. I am so sorry for not putting your shoes on after I put your socks on your feet the night before you died."

I tried to make Ricky go to the hospital but all I was able to do was put his socks on his feet. Ricky was feeling a tightness in his chest and he assumed it was acid reflex. I left home to find a store that was open for the pills he needed to take. I drove around for a half an hour at four o'clock in the morning before and I finally found a store that was opened. I bought him acid reflex pills. For whatever reason, Ricky did not want to go to the hospital. Instead he curled up into my arms for the remainder of the night while I stayed up praying over him to God for comfort and to ease his pain.

I started crying and I said, "I am sorry for working a few minutes later at the office. The office was not as organized as I would have preferred it to be."

I cried so hard that my tears rinsed the soap from my face and left a salty taste on my lips. As I watched the water flow down the drain, I sat numb and dazed in an empty tub. After an hour passed, I grabbed a towel, covered myself, and headed to the computer. I walked into the bedroom to find Ricky's picture on the computer screen staring back at me.

It was as if Ricky was telling me, "I heard every word you said."

The photo reassured me that everything would be fine because he was still with me. Then it hit me. The screen saver that should pop up every five minutes if there is no activity did not pop up. Although I had been in the tub for over an hour, the wallpaper and not the screen saver was on the monitor. I immediately fell to my knees. I crawled over to the chair in front of the computer.

Still crying, I told Ricky, "I'm hurt! I don't know if I can survive this!"

I reached for the computer screen with my left hand. Then I felt like I was lifted and placed into the chair. If I had to identify the lowest point in my entire life, it was at that very moment. I felt so bad that I was not able to save Ricky's life. I did everything I could, but I could not save him. The night Ricky died I was flying into the room when the door opened before me. I did not walk to the telephone and then to him. I flew across the room to get to him. I placed my hands over his heart to help sustain his life and prolong his heartbeat. Instead, his heart beat a final primeval sound echoing far away from me and into the universe. In the solitude of my bedroom, I whimpered when I realized that I was having a conversation with Ricky and it was very real to me. Ricky was there and when my heart felt his presence...

Ricky told me, "Baby, please get up. Everything is going to be okay. I am the lucky one, I am home."

For whatever reason, and to whatever degree, when the struggles of life knock you down to the point that you cannot even pray for yourself, if you allow love to gently touch your heart, love will find a way to lift you up. Sometimes, facing the world can take days, months and even years for love to heal your wounds. Sometimes your heart becomes weaker before it gets stronger.

Lacking the strength in my heart to fully understand what Ricky was trying to tell me, I closed my eyes and then I fell asleep. When I finally woke up, I did not know how many days had passed. Apparently, I slept so long that enough time had passed that I found myself back at Christy's office waiting for my rescheduled appointment. I was very unaware of what was going to happen in this appointment. Unfamiliar with holistic healing, I even worried that maybe it was the Devil's work and I should not proceed with the appointment. If I had to associate holistic healing with something good or bad, then bad was my first assumption because I did not know enough about it to make it "good." When I met Christy, I instantly noticed her angelic features. Her clean and pure spirit gave the room its light. Finally, I was able to lie down on the massage table. The moment I closed my eyes, my spirit removed the windows from the building and let the world come into the room. My spirit replaced the windows with satin white drapes that were so sheer you could see through them like a veil. The drapes were short enough to permit the warm breeze of the summer to move freely into the air-conditioned room. Christy was a "Body Talk" healer who used energy instead of medicine as healing properties. "Body Talk" is an alternative to the traditional medical practice that heals the body from the inside out. Christy told me what she felt my body was telling her about my soul. She saw the image of a gigantic pillar from an Ancient Mayan civilization upright before her. The stone pillar was off toward the side, standing alone like a monument. She felt that I was someone very important like a leader in a tribe. Kristy told me that in my past life, I touched the lives of many people around me. I was Royalty, in a position of authority. Christy felt the excitement from many people from the other side wanting to communicate back to me. I imagined what Christy was saying was true and I was Royalty from a Mayan civilization. Feeling as if I was someone wonderful powerfully lifted my spirits and made me feel strong and special.

My imagination was soaring and started to move a little outside of my comfort zone. I had to immediately open my eyes and look at Christy. Her reaction as she sat next to me on my right side holding my wrist was intriguing. She had chills all over her body as she showed me her goose bumps all over her arms. She told me that she had a wonderful experience treating me. I studied her expression and she truly believed I was Royalty in a past life. Christy told me that I now live my life with authority. I live by structured rules and I still reach out to help many people by inspiring them to do more and good in their life. Then Christy talked about my voice. She said that in my past life I sang to people. I told Christy that it was probably in my past life because I often felt like there was something stuck in my throat whenever I tried to sing. I omitted the fact that I love karaoke. Christy rubbed her hands together and then placed them over my throat. She felt something lodged in my voice box, sort of like a fur ball. She would help me remove it. My appointment with Christy was very fascinating. The information I received in my session resulted in a deeper level of awareness and of clarity of my existence.

When I arrived at home, I had a deeper interest in finding the special person that Christy saw hidden somewhere inside of me. When I turned on my heart channel and I cleared the lines of communication in my mind, I was eager to find out more. Once again, I searched the internet and came across the face of a Mayan tribal leader. When I looked into her eyes on my computer screen, I saw her, La Reina Rojo. It was as if I was staring directly into a mirror looking back at a reflection of myself. Immediately, I felt my soul's connection to La Reina Roja and I was very eager to know more. When the Archaeologists found this Mayan dignitary, they named her the "Red Queen" because she was covered in cinnabar, a scarlet to brick red colored lead with shimmering crystals. The Red Queen was discovered through a secret door in a pyramid in Palanque, Chiapas, Mexico. Inside the pyramid there was a road leading underground to a temple. The Queen was found in the middle room of the temple and was buried inside a solid stone coffin. There were no inscriptions found identifying La Reina Roja. Based on the condition and placement of her burial, she appeared to be Royalty. Today, her history is still unknown. I feel that she is waiting for the perfect moment and very soon the Queen, possibly of a red heart, will reveal her true identity and bring abundant love back into the world.

It was through "Body Talk" that my spiritual side strengthened. I learned my soul loved to travel. Eager to learn more about my culture as well as other cultures around the world. I felt a deep connection to my soul through an invisible umbilical cord that stretched back through a Royal bloodline and possibly to the throne of my soul's first existence.

I continued to encounter spiritual teachers and guides the months following Ricky's death. Another woman that crossed paths with me in a spiritual sense was Colleen, my Yoga instructor. Through Yoga I learned the significance of "Namaste" in Yoga practice. This word or gesture represents the belief of a Divine spark living within each of us which is in the center of our heart chakra. "Namaste" is pronounced at the beginning and end of each Yoga class as an exchange of respect. The meaning of the word "Namaste" brings light when it is spoken. There are various translations in the meaning. My personal translation of "Namaste" is...

"My gift to you is my Divine love.

Please accept my Divine love as a gift and let it sparkle from within you."

This acknowledgement gesture is spoken quietly in the heart from one soul to another. "Nama" means bow, "as" means I, and "te" means you. Therefore, Namaste literally means "bow I you" and translates to "I bow to you." I especially love the level of respect when Namaste is pronounced. It is as if my soul is touched by acknowledging that I can send my Divine love out to the world. At the same time and in synchronicity, I can open my heart to receive Divine love from a new world, a new world that Ricky is now part of and a new way of life that still connects us back to each other.

Ricky's Divine love is sparkling inside of me... "Namaste."

> "There is a road in the hearts of all of us, hidden and seldom traveled, which leads to an unknown, secret place."
> ~ Chief Luther Standing Bear

Sentimiento *(Feelings)*

When your heart is broken nothing else matters. As hard as I tried to move on, there were many times when I was paralyzed and could not cope. Weak and vulnerable, I felt shunned and abandoned by the world. I was lifeless in my own consciousness consumed by predatory grief, a perpetual grief that put me in a state of vertigo and imbalance. The simple instinctive act of waking up in the morning became the most difficult activity for me to master. I hurt from the poisoned spear of separation that pierced my heart, penetrated my spirit and lodged in my soul. I reluctantly opened my eyes each morning and often refused to greet the first rays of light that offered a new day because my new days were empty and void of hope. The faint warmth of sunlight made me feel numb and I chose to stay in bed. I wrapped myself in silk blankets weaving a protective casing much like the caterpillar weaves his cocoon. Staying in bed isolated me from the thievery of a harsh and unfriendly environment. I slept for long periods of time extending into days, living only on the fat stored in my body. I do not recall if or when my feet ever touched the ground. The absence of Ricky's touch was devastating to me. The pain inflicted by being stripped away from a precious and irreplaceable treasure hurt deeply. I retreated to my cocoon. At times tears uncontrollably trailed down my face as I wondered, "Why was Ricky taken away from me?"

I helplessly struggled to live without my beloved Ricky. Persistent feelings of hopelessness overwhelmed me; perhaps it was because I permitted the loneliness to take up refuge in my heart and be integrated within my entire being. Whenever I spoke openly with someone, the topic of my conversation was always Ricky. Over time, my stories became redundant. My friends sincerely intended to listen, but after a few minutes they would find an awkward pause and subtly withdraw. In their best interest, I regretfully changed the channel of my conversation. When in the presence of the not so sensitive, the unsolicited advice seemed to always be the same, "Move on." These two monosyllable words are the most hurtful that one could bestow upon a grieving person. Sadly, the advice did not always come from total strangers. I was extremely disappointed and at times angered at such a lack of concern for my feelings. Each time I heard this advice I felt compelled to shout, "I am NOT ready to move on!" In hindsight, I can offer this to those who are grieving and those who know someone who is grieving. Be genuine. Simple expressions of compassion and sympathy are acceptable and welcomed. When you lose the one you love, you spend countless hours facing the cold windowpane gazing out into the world only to see absolutely nothing. It makes an enormous difference to have people offer sincere heartfelt words; words crafted of pure love. It is okay to recount precious stories and treasured moments about the person who died. It is okay to mention their name. These stories and memories about a loved one are the seeds that must be planted to lift those grieving from the darkness. Crying is healing. The seeds need water too. Trust in your faith that someday the grieving will flourish because they will. Love grows beyond what others may think is the absolute end.

Like the people I came in contact with who did not know what to say to me or how to say it, my thoughts were frazzled too. I so longed for Ricky to be next to me. Through an acute sense of sound, I would strain to hear his voice whisper my name. I would strain to feel the warmth of his breath brush against my neck and delicately land behind my ear. This gave me goosebumps. The pleasurable experience made me whimper and feel once again like the target of perfect love. But when shocked back to reality, my imagination of these tingling kisses abruptly vanished, leaving me alone in the darkness watching the numbers on my alarm clock slowly flip cartwheels for me. Tick, tick, tick; second by second, minute by minute and hour by hour, watching time slowly pass was unbearably agonizing. Ricky's life slipped away in just a handful of seconds. I did not say everything I wanted Ricky to hear because time was not on my side. Losing the love of my life left me with a huge hole in my chest like a crater in the earth. On bended knees I asked for strength and spent countless hours praying to a loving God. My prayers planted me firmly in the present while I found the strength to revisit the past so that whenever I needed to, I could remember and look back at the past with love. When I allowed my heart to open beyond the boundary of grief what I love the most from my past was visible and I knew Ricky could never be lost or forgotten whenever I looked back with love at the past.

In the final seconds of Ricky's life, I held his weary body safely in my arms. Although he was considerably bigger than me, I managed to hold him closely. His head rested securely against my heart. As I caressed his forehead with my kisses, I was calmly speaking to him from my heart; telling him words of love. I know that Ricky was fully aware that I was with him. It was obvious in his facial expression. In an instant he smiled. His smile conveyed a calm and happy message. He was at peace in my arms. Ricky's eyes were normally a dark shade of brown accented with a swirl of an autumn golden hue, but they were different. At that particular moment, when Ricky's eyes landed on my face, they sparkled like brilliant starbursts with light beams bouncing off the walls in the room. This bright light made me feel like I was on stage under a spotlight. The floodgates of light holding back memories of our life together suddenly flung open releasing scenes of our past before me in colorful waves across the room. I saw the Karaoke words flash on the screen the night we met. I saw the flying monkeys in *The Wizard of Oz* and my head buried in Ricky's chest. I saw Ricky standing by the fridge when I caught him in the middle of the night eating a bucket of Neapolitan ice cream. I saw the board games we played, and Ricky score his third Yahtzee; and I saw our private wedding ceremony when we exchanged wedding vows by the old wooden cross.

I reached for Ricky's hand and held it close to my face. I continued to see scenes of our first dance, our first kiss and all the speeches he gave me beginning with, "First of all." The final scene was the last morning we shared together, our final Mananitas. I soon realized that our treasured memories, like sacred chattels, were being collected and were going with him. I looked down at Ricky's face, breathing hard for both of us. As I stared deep into Ricky's eyes, I saw that they were trying to tell me goodbye. His eyes were saying "I love you for life." Time was slipping away faster and faster. I was clinging to every second. Then Ricky's body surrendered his spirit to the enormous white wings that took him away. Somewhere past the double rainbow and beyond the clouds Ricky's spirit faded into the silvery light of Grandmother moon. The room quietly became calm. The scenes had disappeared into the walls. The night was still. I felt a warm chill of affection from that final glimpse that confirmed love's spiritual flight and the amazing power of the soul. The candle keepers of the night sky left a candle burning in the distance to guide me. The flame of the north star burned bright in the night sky in remembrance of Ricky and in proclamation of God's eternal love for me. I often travel the road to the past in search of the sacred chattels. Each time I remember something new and I weave the memory into our story interlacing moments of time. Looking back at our final seconds together always makes me crumble. However, looking back with love makes me feel that Ricky's spirit is alive and is now an integral part of me.

I have a tendency to notice small details around me. One morning not long after Ricky died, I was sleeping at my Mother's house. I awoke to see a gold frame secured to the bedroom wall. The gold accented the unique shape of the frame that enclosed a background of pastel flowers in a stroke of pink blush with the words to The Lord's Prayer resonating in the foreground. I stared at the words focusing on their meanings. "For thine is the kingdom, and the power, and the glory, forever..." Instantly, I felt my heart pump again. Like a child who is eager to speak, I recited each word shifting my gaze from the gold frame on the wall to the gold path up to God. I remembered that Ricky only prayed The Lord's Prayer. He ended all his prayers with The Lord's Prayer. The significance of the prayer to me that morning was that all things begin and end with God. After reading the prayer a few times I made a soulful decision to trust that Ricky's passing was all part of a greater plan. But what was this greater plan? The amazing grace of God's love directed me back to the same course that Ricky and I once set out to discover together. It was time for me to believe in my heart and listen to a greater love that lived inside and all around me. For the first time in a long time I wanted to get up. I wanted to continue the journey Ricky and I started together even if it meant that I was walking alone. I attentively listened to the gentle guidance of Ricky's voice that echoed in my heart. I allowed my heart to open. I felt the sensation of an inner voice hovering over me with the familiar words that Ricky often spoke to me, "You are the love of my life." By listening to my voice repeat Ricky's words over and over, I found my strength and felt the spirit of Ricky's love inside my heart.

I began to experience soulful feelings of Ricky's love nestled inside my being. The memory of Ricky's love brought me back to life. I discovered that I could stand up again, on my own. The love I continued to feel was the ambrosia that nourished my emotional wounds back to health. I delighted in feeling this love. Like sweet nectar at the core of my heart, Ricky's love purified me and baptized me into a new spiritual world. This amazing feeling began to diminish my sorrows. The strength of my spiritual bond with Ricky allowed me to travel freely in the moment without the anxiety of my worst fear, my fear of falling. Then I realized why nectar is the primary constituent ingredient for honey. Love is sweetness. Love emanates full of life when hearts are affectionately intertwined. Love is the rhythm of life, and my love song was recorded to play for my heart. Ricky was my song. I felt the weaves of love from my heart beat rhythmically in and out like musical notes of a sonata and like ocean waves racing to meet the shore.

Somos 4-life

I became sensitized to love's rippling-heart circle effect that drifts across the world in chorus. Despite the force of the tide on life, love can calm and soothe even the toughest waters of life. That is, love can soothe the toughest blows in life like the initial blow you feel when your loved one dies. Love also heals some of the deepest wounds like the gaping wound of being left behind. The old cliché is that time heals. Love also heals. When the claws of grief leave you feeling engulfed by a tsunami, and you have nothing left to give, love will survive the storm and endures the tide.

As I ventured into my new spiritual journey, I thought about how quickly God is to blame when someone dies or when things go wrong. My spiritual journey's theme song was "Bridge Over Troubled Waters" by Simon and Garfunkel. This song took me back to the mornings I shared with Ricky. I could hear his voice. It was a frustrated voice that would roar into the room whenever Ricky's employees habitually called in sick. It was also a voice of defeat because Ricky was left to do the job himself. Occasionally, I witnessed Ricky talking to God, "You kept me alive for all of these years! Why? What more do I have to do for you!" I knew these words all too well. I knew they meant extended hours and that I could expect to see Ricky collapse at the end of the day. I was always saddened by this vision and wanted to help him. Ricky, on the other hand, innately understood our separate responsibilities. I felt so helpless because of my job's demands too. Ricky would always catch the tears that rolled down my face. My tears were wired to Ricky's pain. All I could do was cry. But seeing me cry was the impetus for Ricky to find his inner strength to try to make things better for me, and for us. As for me, I did feel better knowing that Ricky really cared with each tear he caught. Ricky would tell me, "If all I had to do was meet you, then it was worth it."

I may have felt that Ricky knew he was on borrowed time because I would hear him say, "What more do I have to do?" Or, was it that Ricky felt he had so much more time to live because he was finally in love? Ten years before Ricky died, he had a surgical procedure because an artery in his neck was bent causing him to lose blood flow. The severity of the situation resulted in Ricky receiving his Last Rites. Since the surgery, Ricky never understood what it was that he was supposed to do for God in his life but every day for ten years he always asked. Whenever something went wrong, Ricky was at a loss to make it right. Ricky was designed to be overly critical of himself. He was also designed to conquer every obstacle that attempted to knock him down. Ricky told me he was the Captain of his ship. He had a moral and ethical obligation to his ship. He made certain I knew that if troubled waters were to overcome it, he would go down with his ship. The hardships Ricky dealt with in his business were somewhat analogous to going down with a ship in distress. The common thread throughout the hardships was a bridge. A bridge supports and connects. Standing in the center of a bridge can magically suspend you freely in thin air while the bridge offers the support and connection from one side to the other. I disagreed with Ricky wanting to go down with the ship. I thought about bridges and applied them to Ricky. He once worked on the Royal Gorge Bridge when he was young and could visualize this solid structure connecting the masses of land on each side of the Arkansas River. "Ha!" I said sternly. I TOLD Ricky what I felt! God created bridges to be a useful tool. Bridges connect people to places. Bridges remove the physical obstacle and pave the way to reach the desired point. I told Ricky that he had an internal bridge. The internal bridge was the altar of his spirit and soul. Relying on his internal bridge, Ricky had the power, force and the energy to get across safely regardless of what he encountered. A spiritual bridge is one that eternally supports and connects Heaven and Earth. It will never fail. I told Ricky that he was NOT going down with any ship! As the Captain, all Ricky had to do was bring his ship to port. I knew Ricky listened to me because in the end Ricky came home. That memory of troubled waters etched the path for every tear drop to roll down my face from my exhausted eyes. I could have been like any other and blamed God for taking Ricky from me, but I fought this feeling. I tried very hard not to blame God. I asked for help to understand the reason why. It took a long time, but I chose to believe that the meaning of the bridge in the song was significantly more profound than I could have imagined. The bridge was like the hand of God lifting me up so I could walk to the other side and not fall into the pit of darkness. I could suspend myself in the air while I stayed connected to both Heaven and Earth. I thanked God for not letting me go down with my ship, and I thanked God for allowing Ricky to bring his ship home to port and retire it safely before he left this world.

Time slowly passed, second by second, minute by minute, hour by hour, and then day by day. The day before my birthday, about a month after Ricky passed away, I received a phone call from my sister Yolanda. She wanted to record a beautiful life memory and invited me to go with her to the Hot Sulfur Springs. I was very excited and quickly accepted her invitation by shouting, "YES!" into the phone. I knew the hot water would help me feel better. The Hot Sulfur Springs is a very private resort and spa located less than two hours from Denver and tucked away in the mountains near the Winter Park ski area in Colorado. The Hot Sulfur Springs trip would be a welcomed day of complete relaxation. Four of us, Yolanda, our Sister Francis and her friend Cindy and I, hopped into Yolanda's black Rodeo and we were off! Francis and I rode in the back seat of the Rodeo. Separating us was a plump, juicy-red watermelon and a bag stuffed with snacks that Yolanda packed for the trip. The snacks made us so hungry that not long after we hit the road, Francis and I declared that it was time for breakfast. Although Yolanda packed an assortment of snacks, there was only one of each snack. In order to eat what we wanted, Francis and I had to justify to each other why that snack was our favorite. Within seconds our taste buds were indulging in the bite-size chocolate delicacies. We both tried very hard to eat just one snack, but one led to another and yet another. We were like young children making snarky remarks to each other as we attempted to hide our empty snack wrappers. The entire bag of snacks, however, was only an appetizer and did not stop our tummies from grumbling with hunger.

Before we reached the highway that led to the mountains, we asked Yolanda to pull over so we could get some "real" food to eat. We settled into a parking spot directly in front of Camargo's Tamales Restaurant.

Camargo's was also an "old" Mexico shop located near the center of Denver. It had been around for decades and was known for its tamales. An "old" Mexico shop is a smaller version of a grocery/retail store which sells every type of product you can imagine. Crammed merchandise dangles from the ceiling and is piled high across the floor such as an old Mexican favorite, the "piñatas!" And all "old" Mexico shops sell Chiclets (chewing gum in tiny shapes that resemble colorful pillows and have a one second burst of flavor). I remember when I was a teenager, I purchased a pair of concert tickets at Camargo's along with a spit-fire egg and chorizo smothered green chili burrito. Walking into the restaurant set off casual conversations as we reminisced with our "back in the day" girly stories. When we heard the song "Planet Rock" by Afrika Bambaataa jamming on the jukebox, secret stories escaped from our closets and spilled out everywhere. Saying the word Bambaataa was fun and difficult to pronounce if you repeated Bambaataa very fast, we giggled listing to the funny results. The funniest stories were about our big bouncy back in the day hairdos in spiral curls and various shades of purple. My permed hair was gigantic by today's standards! My sister Francis always told me that I could make a crowd part using my big hairdo, just like when Moses used his staff to part the Red Sea. The music that day was an inescapable venture back to our teenage years. We all managed to boogie dance our way out of the Camargo's after we filled up on Mexican cuisine. I can best describe the few minutes we spent in Camargo's as a wonderful, guilt-free feeling of FUN! It was the music from a decade in my life that I referred to as "La Primavera" (springtime) that flourished everywhere that day. The music transported me back to when I was a teenager and when I started to blossom into womanhood. Walking into Camargo's was like opening the closet door of the past. I was able to peak in, look back and be happy! I remembered "feelings" without the shackles of regret of wanting to change my past and start all over again and be different.

After our appetites were satisfied, we hopped back into the Rodeo and continued to our destination. Francis yelled out to Yolanda to turn left so that we could see one of her flower beds. Her small garden creation was right around the corner. Francis worked for the City of Denver as a Horticulturist. Her job was to maintain the gardens in the Denver Parks. Her perennial and annual floral beds were hand crafted; her artistic decor being a stream of beautiful vibrant foliage. The colorful designs captured the visual interest of everyone that enjoyed the pleasure of the landscape. Along the way to the flower bed Francis proudly named all the plants that she had strategically placed in her garden. She further explained how the plants were meticulously positioned so that the smaller, more vulnerable ones were on the outside while the taller, more sturdy ones were in the middle. When we reached the location of Francis' flower bed, we did not see a lush garden of colorful petals and foliage in shades of green. Instead, we saw the crumpled remains of dried flowers and leaves meshed in the dirt. To Francis' dismay, her garden had been destroyed. Francis was so angry. In a voice that pierced the panels of the Rodeo she hollered, "Some fool missed the street and drove right over my garden!" We were all ready to round up a posse and search for clues that would lead us to the carless culprit. Francis failed to understand who could be such an inconsiderate idiot to destroy her beautiful flower bed. I felt so badly for her and even worse when I discovered all the snacks were gone. I could not even offer her a special treat to make her feel better.

After leaving the garden, the rest of the drive was fairly calm, and the mountain scenery was pleasing too. When we reached the resort, a sign out front greeted us with the words, "Please be quiet." I was tempted to remove the sign and make it into a necklace that I could wear to caution oncoming well-wishers. "Please be quiet, I am in mourning." Immediately, I felt the peace of the atmosphere and I was able to soften my heart even more. I permitted the comfort that day would dispatch to enter and rest in my soul. This was my first visit to the resort. I soon discovered the many hot tubs leading up to the top of the mountain. Yolanda told us that the higher you go, the hotter the water. Suddenly, from nowhere, I caught a horrific smell. I caught a whiff of rotten eggs! Yolanda smelled it too and laughed. "Oh yea, by the way, sulfur stinks." The rotten egg smell was from the sulfur springs. The stench of sulfur lingers in your nose but if you hold your nose it seeps into your mouth! Yolanda warned me that I should hold my nose, cover my mouth and take small breaths until I was able to tolerate the smell. A few minutes passed and Yolanda was right. Eventually, I got acclimated to the smell of sulfur and forgot about it. The beauty surrounding me was breathtaking. Finally, I closed my eyes and jumped into the pool. After we were all soothing the tension in our muscles with the hot water, we opened our eyes to find ourselves sitting in a pool of white particles floating everywhere! The white particles were a result of the chemistry of sulfur and sodium in the water. Someone yelled out, "What the hell is that?" Then we all started giggling like little girls who had just made a devilish discovery of pulling out a large pair of panties from their Mother's underwear drawer. Yolanda calmed us down and said firmly, "If your heart is pure, nothing can touch you!" Yolanda's message put us at ease. After all, none of us wanted to admit that our heart was not pure. But for all we knew, we could have been soaking in a life-threatening concoction that was going to seep through the pores of our skin to roast us inside out. We agreed though; if we had to die, the Hot Sulfur Springs was the perfect place to be!

There is a total of 22 baths in different sizes and shapes. The temperature of the healing waters was a controlled range of 95°F to 112°F. Throughout the day we slid in and out of each pool as we climbed higher and higher until we reached the highest and hottest pool. The Hot Sulfur Springs was once the spiritual home of the Ute Indians. The Ute Indians used the element of water to repair their mind, body and spirit. We fit comfortably in our surroundings like four little Indian girls playing in the water, unescorted and having the time of our lives! When we reached the top of the sacred mountain and sat in the highest tub, we saw a majestic eagle fly over our heads, tenacious in spirit. My eyes tracked the eagle to an even higher mountain peak and watched in awe as he built a nest in the Grandfather tree. The eagle's nest was 10,000 feet above the pillars of earth. The enthrallment of witnessing such a beautiful creature in flight and feeling his spirit gently shower protection, strength and healing on me, was truly a blessing that quickly manifested itself into my inner peace. The spirit of the eagle then carried me up like the wind while sheltering me in the shadow of his enormous wings. I was being guided to find tranquility again and the rapture of being alive. The eagle flew above the earth with grace and dignity and over Mount Calgary protecting the Sacred Cross. As I sat in the healing water sweating droplets of grief, I wondered if an eagle could carry special prayers to the heavens. That day, I took a chance, closed my eyes, and trusted the eagle to take and deliver my unanswered prayers. Then, I watched it fly away in a thunderous roar above the mountains.

Undeniably, I was brought to a place where Heaven holds hands with the Earth. Nestled in the middle of nature's masterpiece, I thought about what my life was going to look like going forward. Sulfur is an essential nutrient to health and life that one would die without. Soaking in the sulfur was nourishing my body back to health. I decided it was time to also work on healing my soul. That day, nature's signs were everywhere with important life lessons waiting to be learned. I felt Ricky's strength like, mountains towering over me. The sun was warming my heart from the coldness of death. I began to see, not with my eyes, but with my heart; I began to feel, not with my hands but with my heart; and I began to listen, not with my ears but with my heart.

Life is a gift. Life is a picture. Life is music. Life is seeking and finding love in unusual things not openly disclosed. My love blends into the beauty surrounding me. As I gaze deeply into the blue eyes of the crystal cathedral waters, I can hear music from the river as it echoes the sound of my breath. When the drums of my heart started to beat, I inhale a love song back into my soul. I emerge myself into the magnificent fountain of falling dew. Carefully, I listen to the water whisper its stories about the flow of life reminding me that I must never forget the importance of remembering. When I reach the calm end of the water, I move my fingers around to create ripples in uneven shapes. In admiration of the water's versatility, I wiggle my fingers tips and feel a surge of warmth move through my spine.

Laughter from the girls was the musical soundtrack that would help Yolanda package her gift of creating a beautiful life memory. Then a high-pitched whistle sounded off the side of the road. I saw a train in the distance. As the whistle chirped, I intuitively began to understand my life. The tracks have already been set. The only thing that I must do is stay on the tracks, power forward, and not be derailed. Only I can determine the distance of my travel, and I can go as far as the tracks will infinitely lead me. I envisioned the eagle again. It taught me how to expand the wings of my soul and open my heart so that I may learn everything that God has to teach me. I did just that. Finding a greater strength from within, I was anxious to start working on my Divine life purpose of healing. Like the enchanting eagle, I was anxious to let my spirit travel 10,000 feet higher and spread my wings wider to get closer to God.

I continued to soak in the pool and sat next to Cindy. She listened to my life story about Ricky. I told her that after he passed away, I had to clear his things from the closet. I felt like I was rummaging through his personal items. It was like I was at a garage sale looking for items I wanted to keep and toss. I was intruding, it was uncomfortable, and I felt horrible. I prayed hard the entire time my fingers touched his material possessions. With my eyes closed tightly, I asked God to point me to what Ricky wanted me to have. I stood still waiting to feel the response. Then I remembered reading about how your writing hand is your dominate hand and the opposite hand is your receiving hand. Receiving is a blessing of a gift. I extended my left hand with an open palm toward the ceiling to receive a few of Ricky's personal items that would forever remain with me. I had no idea what I would receive. One by one, I studied the items. Eventually, I received a black t-shirt with the customary alterations that Ricky would make to the sleeves. This black t-shirt stayed on my bed for weeks. One day out of curiosity, I picked it up and unfolded it. I held it up by the corner of each shoulder and stared at the print on the front side of the t-shirt. There was a white number 4 printed inside a white box. I questioned why Ricky would buy a shirt with a number 4 on it. I was at a loss to explain it. I turned the shirt around to see what was on the backside. I saw it! It hit me with the intensity of a one-thousand-watt light bulb. On the backside of the t-shirt printed in solid white letters within a solid white square box was the word... LIFE! I was holding a New World Order (nWo) Wrestling t-shirt. The print on the front and back of the t-shirt had a hidden message for me. When I decoded the message, I read the words "4LIFE." Ricky always included 4LIFE in all his text messages to me. He would end his messages with "I LOV U 4LIFE."

Excited to know more, Cindy interrupted me and asked, "Where is Ricky buried?" I told her, "Florence, Colorado, next to his grandparents." She knew the exact location of the cemetery because her Grandfather was also buried there. I took a second to process what she said recalling a game I played when I was young called "connect the dots." Here is how it works. Take a piece of paper and line up dots in straight columns and rows. The object of the game is to make a square box by connecting four lines. You and your opponent take turns connecting dots drawing one line at a time. When you can make a box by connecting four lines, you put your initials inside the box. In doing so, you score one point. The person with the most points wins the game. When Cindy told me that her Grandfather was buried at the same cemetery as Ricky, I immediately started connecting the dots. However, the square became another tile in an unfolding picture of my Divine life purpose. What I was hearing and seeing was not a coincidence. I was attracting people and things to guide me. Yet, the law of attraction did not apply. There was a deeper more profound meaning. It was the law of desire. I had a desire to reveal answers to my questions. Everything around me was connecting. It was beginning to overwhelm me. It was time for a break.

Being in the water for hours gave our skin the appearance and texture of shriveled up pink raisins, wrinkly and slightly wind burned from the hot temperature of the water. We got out of the pool and dashed away barefoot from the resort to the parking lot, jumping from rock to rock on our tippy toes. Alas, it was time to eat the watermelon! The refreshing pulp and juice of the watermelon was probably the best that I have ever had. We slurped and savored each drop. Then, we caught a chill from the fall breeze that crept over the mountains so we scampered back as fast as we could to the pool area. We retreated into the warmth of the water where we continued to soak and relax for a few more hours. Francis and I were trying to float in the water, but she kept sinking. The weight in her body and not her body weight was very heavy. I tried to help her by placing my hands below her back, but she was like an anchor determined to sink to the bottom. I wondered what it was that weighted her from within. We continued to share our secret girl stories and created a moment that we could talk about for the rest of our lives. Yolanda's mission was accomplished! We were all very happy just being together. The day at the Hot Sulfur Springs was the most amazing day in my spiritual journey. I gave myself a few hours to escape from my pain and embrace life. This was the day that I woke up from the initial shock of my grief because I allowed myself to connect above, below, around and within to the warmth of God's love.

Ricky's love reminded me when life is embraced you will find love.

> "We do face the sun and pray to God through the sun,
> asking for strength to complete the Sun Dance,
> and that our prayers will be heard, and in the sun, we see visions."
> ~ Frank Fools Crow

Mañanitas *(Mornings)*

Healing is a personal journey when meaningful life lessons unfold in the mind, heart and soul. At times there is conflict causing life's direction to become confusing and challenging, especially in grief because this is when a person is most vulnerable and weak. When I was grieving my Mother told me, "You can live your entire life but if you are not living your *own* life, then you don't have a life." My Mother was right. I had to move beyond the pain and rise above the surface of grief to reclaim my life. In doing so, I learned that my heart was not as fragile as I once believed. However, life is. Life is fragile and precious; and so is time.

The Hot Sulfur Springs was a sacred place for me. It was a place where I felt guarded by the goodness of nature's domain. It was also a place where I felt the immense sadness swelling inside my heart. I felt robbed by Ricky's death. I felt cheated of the life that I should have had with Ricky. Ricky and I should have grown old together. Instead, we were separated by death. I was hurt and my heart was heavy. At the same time, there was a determination that tugged at my heartstrings telling me to find a way to escape the imprisonment of anger, guilt and resentment. I did not want my spirit to be conquered and sucked into the grooves of the cold canyon walls. Surrounded by the beauty of nature's backdrop, I felt the strength of Ricky's spirit. I felt Ricky in the mountain, and he was telling me, "Stand up! Don't give up without a really good fight!" I had no choice but to honor

Ricky's words and comply with the message I received. I had to fight. I had to be brave like a wounded warrior and confront what could ultimately defeat me. One by one I faced the anger and guilt of grief; the resentment and bitterness of loss; the abandonment and loneliness of death. I fought these feelings and so many more to evict them from my heart. I silently attacked the emotional sadness and permitted the overwhelming agony deep within my soul to spill over the mountains and send my piercing cries echoing throughout the canyon. When I was finally emancipated from my sorrow, I asked my heart for forgiveness and received the eagle's feather for courage. Being released from my burdens was like the flesh of my soul being exfoliated against the rocks at the base of the mountain. I felt raw. Oddly, I was healing. Committed to only the love rooted in the atrium of my heart, I had faith that victory was mine. I lifted myself up from my despair and tenderly cradled the pieces of my broken heart in the palms of my hands. I felt lighter after shedding the bitterness that brought me down. Triumphantly, I shouted at the mountain, "Ricky, I won! I did it! I did it for love!" Inspiration charged my spirit to the top of the mountain like an electrical surge rushing to the star on the top of a December evergreen. I entrusted the eagle with undeniable authority to fly away clutching my most precious prayers then watched it glide across the endless azure sky. God's voice was pounding everywhere; in the water, in the breeze, and in the sun. I could see it. I could feel it. In the freshness and purity of the pristine waters, my spiritual life was reborn. I inhaled a hint of rosemary from the ponderosa pine. The sun delivered a heartwarming greeting to the earth with its infusion of pure light that could touch the entire world eternally. The trees around me smiled. Their celebratory approval of my achievement had a rippling effect on my spirit. A whirling energy formed circles within me beginning at the base of my spine then weaving itself in and out of my heart as if I was a garment in the hands of a tailor. The seamless stitches of golden thread were mending me so that my heart would never feel broken again. I was healing.

I was finally able to relax in the Hot Sulfur Springs. I exhaled slowly and deeply releasing a mist of air from my mouth. Bending over to investigate the chalky water I focused on my lungs and exhaled all impurities from my life. The sulfur washed away the gloom and cleansed my mind. I drenched my spirit in the water's life force. I started to feel the warmth of love as I admired the sun in its golden, radiant beauty. My mind and heart were in balance and I was at peace. I opened my soul and studied its path along my journey. When my diaphragm regained its normal rhythm, I felt as if life was waiting for me to breathe again. I reached out to grasp the water, but it slipped through my hands. As wonderful as the water felt, I knew it was impossible for me to sit in it forever. Water moves. I had to move. My direction was changing. I would find my way just as I found my own journey. After spending a day at the Hot Sulfur Springs, I decided never to become lost in one of life's corn mazes. By taking control and changing direction, my soul was illuminated with the grace of life and gratitude of peace. I realized that my being was an integral part of the earth, water and air. Love permeated the thin veil between the material world and the spirit world and connected me to the serenity of the other side.

Exhausted from the spiritual awakening at the Hot Sulfur Springs, I returned home with plans to sleep like a bear in hibernation. I slipped into a night shirt, lugged my body across the room to my bed and pulled back the crisp white cotton sheets. Alone in the shadows of the welcoming night, I crawled underneath the blankets and pulled them over my head. I enjoyed breathing again and caught the smell of lemongrass laundry detergent. The scent opened an airway in the back of my throat and cleared my nose of the rotten egg smell from the sulfur in the water. I yawned and fervently gulped some more fresh air into my lungs then stretched my arms outward as wide as possible. Finally, I was ready to retire into my dreams.

It was late in the evening and the night was very dark. Ironically, in absolute darkness I could feel light. A shimmering stream of light skewered my bedroom. I felt drawn to it. Aimlessly, my eyes searched the room for the source of this light. Could it be that I left a candle burning in the adjacent room? I cautiously sat up in my bed. Then I noticed it. The light was coming from the warmth of water still clinging to my skin from earlier that day. The water stayed with me. I was amazed at how the light gave the appearance that I was glowing in the dark. My aura was generating waves of light inside my bedroom, from within me. With a stroke of love, a painter's brush carefully touches the canvas to create a special image. Similarly, resonating with love, I was touched by my Maker with a splash of water to give me a special glow. Before I drifted off to sleep, I reconnected with God in an intimate prayer to give Him thanks. I spoke of the healing waters and of my spiritual triumph. Water is clear and, in its transparency, I understood the message it delivered that day. I learned that joyful memories with people I love are the most precious gifts and priceless treasures that a heart could ever possess. These memories are the vivid impressions of my life displayed within my being and sealed with God's signature on the canvas of my soul. Ricky taught me to cherish our memories because they are classics. Just like the memory of the night we stayed up to watch *The Wizard of Oz*. That night was our first classic that Ricky recorded for me inside my heart. For the rest of his life Ricky gave me a collection of classics of his love. I could not sleep anymore. The Hot Sulfur Springs were like a stimulant to my senses, even better than a caffeine jolt. My spirit was massaged by the healing element of the water. I was energized and wanted to stay up all night to remember my classics. I played the special memories stored in my heart repeatedly well into the early dawn until I finally drifted off to sleep.

I awoke that next morning with an insurmountable sensation of love. I could still feel the bond between the sun and the mountain at the Hot Sulfur Springs where all was one in spiritual harmony. I thought about my favorite bath at the peak of the mountain where the eagles nest. It was a place where the sun stepped down from the sky to bestow a kiss on the jewels that glistened from beneath the halos of the mountain tops. Could it be that I was sitting in the exact place where Heaven's light reaches down to christen the earth? Or was it the light of my spirit that yearned so hard to reach up and touch Heaven? Quite possibly, it was the distinct place where the sun paused to recharge its power. It was that place where I found my strength. It was the same place where I learned the significance of loving ourselves first. When we love ourselves first, we honor our heart. By honoring our heart, we respect life. And when we respect life, there is love. Ricky's love for me was an imperishable spirit and the light of the sun showed me love has no boundaries, borders, and no end. Perhaps, that is why I still love Ricky. Our love stems from the root of an infinite light like the light of the early morning or "Mañanitas" which gives the world hope with the dawn of a new day, every day.

The Mañanitas are a cycle of life when Mother Earth reveals her exquisite beauty and shares with the world a majestic sun. As the rays of the morning light stretch across the horizon, the sky is caressed with a blend of soft colors that blossom together in complete perfection. The color of the morning sky soothed my soul and helped me ease into my day. I learned that if I receive the Mañanitas with love and an open heart, the entire day may be filled with many, many blessings. While the tranquil light of the Mañanitas is at its peak for only a moment briefly each morning, in my spiritual development, I experienced her light over a prolonged period every morning. The light brought a message of hope and helped me find my inner strength and wisdom so that I no longer isolated myself from others. By opening my heart, I was opening my life to receive new daily blessings. Healing occurs for everyone in different ways. For me, I believe it was through light that I became the emissary of my own love. Light is the emanation of celestial power and an Almighty God. With light, I had salvation and a promise of a new day. Light gave me back my life and a chance for a new beginning with many blessings that were still to come.

Waking up in the morning became the most important part of my day. I made it a ritual to wake up and greet the Mañanitas. I took advantage of every moment of this quiet time to search for a higher vision. My thoughts traveled beyond my being to express sincere thanks and deep gratitude, but most of all, to see an inner beauty. For me, the Mañanitas evoked a time for prayer and for love. In the morning I would think of Ricky. I would imagine that the sun's rays were his arms protruding from the sky to reach out to me and wake me up. The sun became this masculine being kneeling before me compelled to brush light upon my face just as Ricky used to express his love to me with his benediction for a safe return home. Loving Ricky this way fueled my heart to pump and made loving a manifestation of life itself. The warmth of the sun helped me remember love and made me feel excited about being in love again. The morning sun was a vivid reminder of the love that survived inside my heart. When I nurtured love, I felt Ricky. Love never abandoned me. Ricky wanted me to sustain his love in my heart. In fact, it continued to grow when I was grieving, when I was all alone and whenever I slept my life away.

As light shines on life it reveals the sparkle and vitality of the spirit. It also reveals the blemishes and imperfections of the mortal being. Like stubborn stains on white satin, these spots are impossible to scrub clean and difficult to conceal. The spots on my being made me feel old and worn and represented the dark moments in my life that I tried hard to forget; the disturbing feelings that I tried hard to avoid; and the defective thoughts that I tried hard to tuck away in the corners of my mind. In light there is no shrouded secrecy, only truth. When my spiritual light was turned on, the many impurities in my life that needed cleansing were painfully visible. My Mother did not tolerate the most microscopic speck of dirt and dust in her home. We call her the "Queen of Clean" because her house is always spotless. My being, the home of my heart, spirit and soul, needed to be spotless like my Mother's house. There was so much work to be done I struggled with where to begin. When reaching for the soap and a bucket of water I thought about how Ricky's profession was based on his pride for getting carpet back to factory-fresh clean. I never had a chance to go to a work site with Ricky although I remember frequently asking him if I could tag along. Ricky never let me go with him. I do not know why. He managed to keep me at a distance, in a place where I needed to be so that I could experience my own lessons in life. Through his unconscious practices, Ricky taught me that the most important battle I had to fight was against one enemy. That enemy was me. Ricky knew that the person inside me was far better than ordinary and that with love, I could be extraordinary. Since Ricky's death, I have learned to differentiate the ordinary person I was from the extraordinary person that Ricky knew I could be.

Most of my learning experiences came from signs and messages I received well after Ricky died. I translated signs and messages into something beautiful and meaningful that I could hold inside my heart. If I continued to feel the uplifting light of the Mañanitas, I knew I was on the right path of learning my life lessons as I began to understand the significance of each sign and each message. I learned how to communicate from my soul and be open to what the world was trying to teach and tell me. One day while working in my yard a sign came to me in the form of a long skinny green bug that looked like a long blade of grass and the grass had huge bulging alien-like eyes. I made eye contact with this little creature and I was able to decode its meaning. A Praying Mantis has unusual long limbs that appear as if the arms were in a praying position, thus the insect's name. This insect was a sign that prayer from the depth of my soul to a loving God is a powerful lifeline to who I am and who I can become. This insect brought a message to me that I can find answers to life's questions hidden within the grooves of my soul if I prayed and made prayer a part of my daily life. There was so much in this world waiting to teach me when I listen with my heart. There is meaning in every experience and in every experience, there is a balance of forces at any given time. The forces, like the yin and the yang, opposite but at the same time complementary to each another. Both interact in a dynamic system and comprise a greater whole. The yin and yang provided a lesson in considering the two forces of good and bad together. The bad is often construed as evil or negative energy and to balance the force of bad there is good. Bad is complementary to good. I now think of bad in a positive sense. Something that exists in the bad can be converted to a good resulting in a positive life lesson. Without bad, life lessons are not as obvious and life lessons may never be learned. I used the concept of yin and yang to start breaking down the conflicts in my own life.

By understanding the bad, I could find its complement, the good, in order to find the best solution and attain the right life balance in my own life.

Numerology-related signs and messages also surrounded me during the initial days of being alone. I became fascinated with numbers and was curious to learn the meaning behind all numbers or combination of numbers. I saw beyond the number and studied it basic shape and symbolic reference. The number three seemed to bring a strong message as it surreptitiously appeared and reappeared before and after Ricky died. Ricky and I saw three people during what turned out to be Ricky's final birthday dinner. I served Ricky three slices of birthday cake on his birthday. I saw three rainbows before Ricky died. Three people stood over Ricky's body to say The Lord's Prayer. Three rocks inexplicably fell out of a red glass vase and into my hands when I was packing to move; one of them being the rock Ricky added to the vase. What was the message in the number three? When you look at the number 3 it is shaped like an open heart that stumbled on its side. I saw the number three as a symbol of love. In Biblical scriptures the number three is the first of four perfect numbers and represents "completion." Three is known as Divine; three marks Divine completeness and perfection. The number three most importantly represents The Father, The Son and The Holy Spirit or The Holy Trinity. Equally significant is that the number three is a definition of time; it is the past, the present, and the future.

As I continued to analyze the meanings behind signs and messages, I became like Helen Keller after she was introduced to communication by her teacher Anne Sullivan. I was like a child demanding and wanting to know more outside of what I was taught. Thus, I opened my heart to the meaning of color. The night Ricky passed away I blindly packed a few items before leaving to my Mother's house. I did not consciously pack. I went through the motions without emotion. I took Ricky's red Jordan hoodie and an oversized pillow stuffed in a red pillowcase. When I arrived at the familiar house on the hill, my Mother had prepared my old bedroom for my retreat. That night I remember seeing a hazy, rose colored light appearing on the white bedroom wall. The red light could have come from the taillights of a car backing up into a driveway, although I did not hear the engine of a car. The light was soft yet luminous and very soothing. Red is described in the Scriptures as representative of Divine love. Red is the universal color of Valentine's Day. Red is the color of a bull fighter's cape, the bullfighter that Ricky told me he always wanted to be. Red was the color of Ricky's pillow that I grabbed when I left the scene that changed my life forever. Red was a message like the number 3 that I was, I am, and I will always be... loved.

Death can leave a constant feeling of being physically cold to those living through loss. Although Ricky died in the middle of summer, I was easily chilled. I countered the cold by chasing the warmth of the sun. Three days after Ricky passed away, I followed a sunset. The sun was so beautiful I was lured to the side of the road where I parked the car to stop and stare at its grandeur. I reached for my camera phone to capture the moment and took several photos. The next day I loaded the photos to my computer. I was amazed at what I captured. Every photo showed wisps of radiant red patches positioned around the sun. I studied the photos as I anxiously pounded the keyboard doing searches on the Internet to explain the phenomenon. I came across some information about orbs. An orb is a common anomaly of dust particles in the camera lens that creates the ghostly white, red, yellow and green circular images in a photo. Some people think dust particles are spirits that appear as lights in photos. I thought I was just taking pictures of a beautiful sunset. The images captured in the photos were evidence of so much more. When I stared at the last photo, a brilliant red orb was strategically positioned next to the sun. The sun appeared as a bright star and the red orb looked like a bullfighter's cape. It was a sign! I felt the consoling message of that red orb. Against the glow of the descending sun, the orb, like a red bullfighter's cape, was Ricky's cloak to comfort me and tell me everything was going to be okay.

During my journey I did not always consciously look for signs. At times, I was aware of them only when they jumped out at me, after the same symbol appeared repeatedly over and over again until it finally got my attention. Other times I purposely looked for signs and in some cases I was unable to decode them. I often played a numbers game along my route to work to seek out signs and decode their hidden messages. It was like hunting Easter eggs to fill my Easter basket; instead, I was hunting for that special gift to put in my heart's treasure box. The gift, like the Mañanitas, would bring light and hope into my day. While driving to work I studied the letters and numbers of license plates on the cars around me. Before I could make any sense of what I noted, a message would come to me that captured how I was feeling. One morning when I was feeling very sad and down and needed to feel love, two licenses plates seemed to wave at me and call my attention to them. The first license plate was on a car and had the numbers 411. The second license plate was on a truck and had the letters MSU. I instantly unraveled and understood the message. The three numbers "411" are universally understood to mean *information*; that is, 411 is a way of communicating or providing information. The information was "MSU".

> The special gift I received that morning was the message "MSU" meaning "MiSs U".

My spiritual guides were everywhere and in everything. They gently nudged me forward in life when my heart was weak but still willing to acknowledge them and the information they delivered. One of my spiritual guides was my Mother who embodied exceptional strength. I had long conversations with my Mother about the feelings deeply rooted in the sanctuaries of our hearts. She shared with me her account of walking up the stairs to the second level of her Victorian home. Built in the 1890s, the red brick walls of the humble house on the hill supported the mystical memories of generation, after generation of families passing in and out of its structure. My Mother knew every corner of the house and could navigate the stairs blindfolded. Bracing the solid banister worn with the handprints of so many young and old, weak and strong, my Mother slowly ascends step by step. With each step she takes she focuses on talking to my Grandmother and my Father who passed away as if they are waiting for her at the top of the stairs. My Mother tells them she will get there when she is "good and ready", meaning she has a choice and chooses not to leave her family just yet because she loves her life. When my Mother is finally upstairs, she spends time alone with the man from Mexico she married years ago and the Mother she cared for faithfully. But she is alone. My Mother shared with me her sadness of being over eighty years old and experiencing the deaths of so many people she loved. Step by step she always managed to move forward in her life even when the heartache was too heavy to bear.

My Mother's most touching story was about the death of her cousin. This person was raised by her maternal Grandmother and had a difficult childhood. She was the subject of the jokes by my Mother's seven brothers and the other cousins. Despite her cousin growing up without much parental direction, this cousin had a very cheerful outlook throughout her life. In her adulthood, she enjoyed being with anyone and was genuinely happy. One day my Mother received a telephone call that this cousin who lived in another state was very ill and near death. In the final hours of her cousin's life, my Mother described how she was gifted the ability to help her cousin leave this world. Alone in the solitude of her home, my Mother imagined herself at her cousin's hospital bedside. She felt a very fine silk veil over her head and felt the veil being tenderly lifted. As the veil was lifted, my Mother raised her arms with her cousin's soul resting peacefully in the palms of my Mother's hands. With fully extended arms, my Mother lovingly released her cousin's soul into Heaven. The next day my Mother learned that her cousin had died. The news confirmed what my Mother already knew.

My spiritual journey was exhausting. My spirit was growing fast in knowledge and strength and I felt that my spirit no longer fit my body with the overflow of the signs and messages I received. I continued to oversleep. Occasionally, whenever I had the energy, I would take a walk. When I was thirsty, I drank water, and when I was hungry, I ate. Functionally, I was living but emotionally, I struggled. Sometimes, I would have an odd craving like the day I craved a thick juicy hamburger. Kieko, invited me to have lunch at the restaurant where he worked so I jumped at the invitation to spend time with my son. It was a welcomed reason to get out of the house. I grabbed my car keys and I rushed out the door. When I arrived near the restaurant I had to drive around a few blocks before I finally found a metered parking space. The rumbling of my famished stomach was so loud and distracting I did not feel or hear the tires rub when I parked too close to the curb. I was trying hard to pay attention that day. Quite possibly, I was trying too hard, so I stopped to take a deep breath and relax. After I got out of the car my legs were on auto pilot and directed me to the restaurant.

The restaurant was also a bowling alley located on the third level of the Denver Pavilions off 16th Street Mall in downtown Denver. Two separate escalators stretch from the street up to each floor. From the second level the next escalator requires a small jaunt around the first elevator to get to it. I walked through the Pavilions with my head down hoping to find a penny, one with the head facing up to give me good luck. My eyes were still fixed on finding the penny as I stepped onto the escalator. I watched each step unfold and felt myself being carried away. When I reached the third level, I placed my hand on the rail to step off the escalator, I noticed something to my right. I turned to find myself standing directly in front of a Blue Bridal Boutique. Like a slap in the face I was immediately reminded of my wedding plans that would never materialize. I drifted to the bridal shop window and put my hands on the glass. Through the haze created by my breath on the glass, I envied the mannequin cloaked in the long white crystal-like gown who seemed to be staring back at me in pity. But all I could think about was Ricky telling me that he did not want monogrammed towels in the bathroom, and I wondered why. Time stopped while I stood there draped in my emotion of never being able to wear the dress. I told God all I wanted was to find a lucky penny. Before my tears could fall, I remembered my wedding! Ricky and I were married in a very private and personal ceremony before God and no one else. Our commitment to each other was sealed on the very day we exchanged our vows. I did not need a white wedding dress to make me beautiful. The love in Ricky's eyes made me feel amazing and so very blessed by His Divine love. I peeled my face from the glass and took a few steps back. I could see a smile in the reflection of the window. It was my smile and the white light all around me made my spirit soar. I received an important message that day I set out for a hamburger. The message was that I may not always get what I ask for, but I will always have what I need. I asked God for something so insignificant like a penny for luck. What I received was a bridal store and another memory of Ricky. God's message was that I did not need to find a penny for luck. The bridal store reminded me that I was already lucky in finding love.

Because I slept a lot, I dreamt a lot and my dreams were usually good dreams with nothing that frightened me. Most of my dreams were vivid with some type of story attached. During one of my frequent naps I had a dream of a beautiful albino snake. The snake was slithering up a spiral staircase; the stairs were lined in red royal velvet. Once at the top of the stairs, the snake was at my eye level. It gave me an electrifying surge of energy that felt powerfully magnificent! I reached down to touch the snake behind its head but suddenly I threw it into a river to be free. I am not certain why I threw it, as a matter of fact, this disturbed me after I woke up. I queried the word "snake" on the Internet. Naturally, the search engine returned a plethora of information. I scanned the results until I found a picture of a snake like the snake in my dream. It was an albino white ball python, a very docile snake. It can appear to be shy and is very reluctant to bite. The snake was dubbed the name ball python because of its habit of curling into a ball when threatened. I was like this snake in that I would shy away from conflict. I was eager for an interpretation of my dream. I spent countless hours researching snake dreams and made several trips to the library for different dream books and books on snakes. What was the meaning of my dream and why did the snake appear? I read that snake dreams are very powerful messages and should not be feared. Snakes have the unique ability to shed their old skin and refresh themselves with a new outer layer of skin. In this respect, snake dreams symbolized my own individual's spiritual awakening and spiritual growth which is what I had been experiencing since I lost Ricky.

From my research I learned about the Kundalini, in Hinduism it is a form of Divine energy at the base of the spine. The Kundalini is depicted in Indian scriptures as Shakti, a Serpent Goddess that possesses a supernatural force of energy. The Goddess in me was awake. Another night I woke up from a dream when I felt a tremendous surge of power. I had never experienced such a feeling. The force of energy was an intense power that I may never feel again. It felt like a sweet kiss on my soul that opened like a doorway. I woke up feeling this burst of energy. I ran to my computer and quickly turned it on with a determination that surprised me. This was the very night that I designed my book cover and my story was born. I quickly wrote down all the chapters and my love for Ricky unfolded right in front of me like musical notes every time my fingers tapped away at the keyboard. The letters and words were passionately freed from the depth of my heart.

Focused on a spiritual awakening, I worried that my job would interfere with me finishing my book and being able to share my story. However, when it is time to complete life's journey it does not matter what obstacles are in the way, there will be signs to help overcome them. When I really needed these signs, they were there. On August 19, 2011 one month after Ricky's death, I drove to work feeling the claws of grief gripping me the way my hands gripped the steering wheel. I did the only thing I could do and that was to pray. I asked God for three gifts: spiritual guidance, a message, and a sign. I arrived at the office, sat down at my desk, and began to open the day's email. The first email I received was from my Wellness Coach, Sabrina, whom I found through my employer sponsored wellness program. Every three months I established my wellness goals with the assistance of a Wellness Coach to live a much healthier life. Sabrina played a key role in my journey because she documented many of my stories that depicted my mental and physical state over several years. I spoke to Sabrina the previous day and told her I felt that I needed to be doing more. I was being driven to do something special, something significant, but I did not know what specifically. I told her I carefully took note of the signs I received and was listening intently, but I still did not know what my Divine life purpose was, and she was not aware of my "snake" dream. The first gift in response to my prayers came from Sabrina. She gave me the name of a Spiritual Guide or Akashic Reader. An Akashic Reader interprets a person, who they are and what their purpose is in life. The second gift that day came when I picked up my postal mail from the office mail room. I received a package containing some reading material sent by the hospital's bereavement coach, Geri. She gave me a beautifully illustrated book titled *Tear Soup* and several pamphlets on grief and healing. She was an exceptionally good listener, a necessary trait in her line of work. Geri rescued me from the office with an invitation to lunch. I believe that Geri's package was the message that I prayed for as it was a blessing to receive that day.

I tried to keep my eyes and heart open wide in anticipation of receiving the third gift, a sign, as I knew it would come just like the other two gifts. I left the office to get lunch with one of my colleagues, Tanna, whom I had worked with for more than five years. The Children's Hospital is located north of Colfax Avenue that runs east and west intersecting the city of Denver. The office is located on the south side of Colfax, across the street from the hospital. Tanna and I decided to take a walk and get lunch at the hospital. When we crossed Colfax, we were greeted by a procession line coming toward us. I had just a few seconds to dart across the sidewalk and cut through the procession line. As I was running, my eyes were magnetically drawn to a figure at the center of the procession. My heart started to pound like a drum, and I was able to clearly see every detail of that day. I could sense the energy of people around me but could only see her. She was huge and appeared to be descending from the sky. "She" was a statute of a benevolent Saint clothed in black and was being carried on a stretcher type platform. Although she was only a statue her spiritual existence appeared to be very life-like. Perhaps, it was the energy that emitted from the people surrounding her that made her seem real. Each time I closed my eyes and opened them again I could feel my tears fall yet I was not crying. The palms of her slender hands were joined together in a prayerful gesture and positioned firmly in front of her heart. Her frail hands were clasped together and sculptured to capture the beauty of her delicate veins. Every one of her thin little fingers stretched upward toward the sky in tribute to His love. I was drawn to her pure and innate spirit as I felt her compassion and sincere loyalty to her faith radiate upon her face. Her presence was a signal to calm me down while I reached for an infinite peace from within. As I stared into her compassionate eyes, I told myself, "If this is not my sign, then what is it?" Suddenly an older woman emerged from the group and approached me. She had at least fifty plastic rosaries draped over her arms like a shawl and held several more in her hand that glistened in the August mid-day sun. This woman asked me if I could use a rosary and I immediately answered, "Yes! Yes, I can use a rosary! Thank you so much!"

I believe that everything happens for a reason, so I had to know the reason why the procession line was on Colfax at the very moment I had to cross the street. In my research I learned that August 19th is Saint Sarah's feast day, a day when a statue of Saint Sarah is carried in an annual procession (typically toward the sea) as a reenactment of her arrival in France. Saint Sarah (pronounced Sare-ah) is also known as Sara-la-Kali which means Sarah the black. The word *"black"* is in reference to her dark skin color. Sarah is a Black Madonna. The information I read about Sarah indicated that she was amazingly beautiful. Some stories refer to her as the Cinderella of her time. Saint Sarah had visions that she must help Mary Magdalene, Mary Jacobi and Mary Salomé even before they arrived on the shores of France in a small boat without oars and without a sail. Some claim the Holy Grail was with them on their journey. The three women were carrying good news of Christianity tucked safely inside their hearts. The three Marys survived because they had a story to tell and their story had to be written. Perhaps, because I survived an unbearable heartbreak, I too had a story and my story had to be written.

Since 1999, members of the Mission of St. Isidore Roman Catholic Church in Watkins, Colorado have embarked their faithful congregation on a 50-mile walk to the mountain home of Mother Cabrini Shrine in Golden, Colorado. This was their two-day pilgrimage honoring the Kingship of Christ and the Triumph of the Immaculate Heart of Mary. Parishioners give thanks to Mother Cabrini for her intercession in the completion of their beautiful church of St. Isidore in Watkins. The pilgrimage provides confession, reflection of a new spiritual direction, meditation, and a group rosary prayer time. My spiritual journey crossed paths with the parishioners of the Mission of Saint Isidore Roman Catholic Church on the streets of Colfax Avenue in Denver, Colorado. Crossing the path with this spiritual group of people directly in front of Children's Hospital reminded me of the following Bible passage:

> "even the darkness will not be dark to you;
> the night will shine like the day,
> for darkness is as light to you."
> Psalm 139:12

Darkness is not dark to me. Darkness and light are the same. Like the Mañanitas that give light to the new day, the moon and the stars give light to the night. It is the intricate balance of the universe, the yin and the yang. When I thought about the moon it may have been that Ricky wanted me to know the moon was there the night before he died because there are no outlines that separate death from life, life from time or love from its lover. Light is a symbol that reminds me of love. Love that will always live in my life when there is darkness all around me. When light dwells inside my heart, I will never live in darkness again.

The Immaculate Heart is a devotional reference to Mary's inner heart that is filled with joy, sorrow, virtue, compassion, and grace. The Immaculate

Heart will triumph. People who completely surrender their heart will receive Mary's powerful love. Collectively, hearts that beat with genuine and pure love of the Immaculate Heart will ignite an amazing love throughout the world, like a golden sunrise across the endless sky.

My journey of healing began when I set out to mend my broken heart. As my heart opened, a new world came into view and taught me many life lessons that I needed to know to overcome the difficulties of understanding grief. Learning to live again is like painting a portrait of knowledge with a powerful stroke of love. The portrait is a journey of life tucked away deep inside the soul that is hand painted with all of the beautiful colors of love that adorn the heart.

I believe the most powerful element of healing one's heart is through love.

> He refreshes my soul.
> He guides me along the right paths
> for His name's sake.
> Psalm 23:3

Razones *(Reasons)*

It was important for me to remember my soul mate. I hope the memory I have of him never dies. I would like to believe that Ricky did not die. I would like to think that Ricky too had a life journey. In his journey, Ricky has taken his last walk to the top of life's highest mountain and he proudly stands at the peak looking down at me, happy to see how he contributed to my life. Ricky is everything in me. His many lessons taught me that I could see past my pain.

Although grief is a traumatic life experience the greater promise of peace brings forth the signs of Heaven on Earth. Perhaps that makes surviving grief some sort of miracle. I never reached a point in my life where I could proclaim, "Yes, I finally moved on! Yes, I am finally over losing Ricky!" I searched for the feelings and sifted through the words but failed to find them. I failed to move beyond my life partner who stood beside me on my worst hair day and easily made me believe I was adorably beautiful. I failed to get over losing my soul mate who decided the only place in the world he wanted to be before he left this earth was inside my arms. Ricky is irreplaceable and my heart will always feel his void. Ricky changed my life. Yet, I found my strength and I can say that the piercing pain of Ricky's death slowly subsided. There is something magical about pure love that refuses to die. It is like sharing that final goodbye and saying hello all within the same breath. Living through grief has taught me invaluable, meaningful life lessons that transformed me into the person that I was destined to be. Gradually, when the fog of grief lifted, I was able to let my heart smile again.

The night before Ricky died, he felt the light of the moon gently touch the side of his face through a small crack in the Venetian blind. Ricky told me that I let the moon into our bedroom and into our life. The moon had a significant meaning and Ricky wanted me to take special note of it. Long after Ricky's death I continued to think about the moon but could never decipher its message. Then one summer night during a stroll outdoors the message came to me. Standing alone in stillness, I felt the air-brushed coolness against my face as I gazed up at the countless stars plotted against the infinite darkness, their light beams were shining down on me. Standing in the brightness of their light, like an amateur karaoke performer frozen in the spotlight, I stood captivated with my eyes fixed on the ceiling that was night. Among the many stars in a plethora of sizes, brightness and clusters, the mysterious Waning Gibbous moon appeared directly above me. I was the main attraction of the stage. Unlike the moon phase that appeared the night Ricky died; this Waning Gibbous moon had a more vibrant appearance. It had a peculiar personality. It had a chivalrous charm. And it had a smile. The slight arch of the humpback moon resembled a simpering, almost conceited smile. It sparkled at me displaying its mischievous amusement as it showed me some very big teeth followed by a long, smirky grin as if to remark, "Nanc, what took you so long?" I often wonder, was that Ricky in the moon? That brilliant, beautiful moon was everything but waning as it smiled my tears away.

Memories of the deceased are healing stories for those in grief. Unsolicited expressions of remembrance reveal personal accounts that are sacred to those who yearn to keep the memory alive. Collectively, the stories and scenes become the quilted pattern of life in the past tense. When carefully stitched together the quilt transforms into a colorful wrap of warmth and comfort for the broken hearted. Memorial gatherings offer a glimpse of past pivotal moments that merge the living with the dead. Like a bittersweet kiss bestowed tenderly on the weakened soul, memorials can bring the dead to life and give life back to those already living. Throughout this exchange, grief imprints its energy on the soul in whatever form it elects to display at any given moment; denial, anger, bargaining, depression or even acceptance. The deeper the love, the deeper the grief will be. Growing up in a large extended family I was not unfamiliar with death but had a different perception of it. I used to think that memorial services and family gatherings were limited times to talk about the person who died, express final good-byes and then bury the deceased's existence forever. Death is so much more. Dying is an act of taking and giving. Death steals from you. It rips into your being and takes what can never be replaced. In return, death gives a vision beyond mortal existence to those who open their hearts to the journey. In grief, love can seep into the soul and turn the heart like a wheel in motion. When a heart is in motion, the spirit acts as if it had wings of the air. When the spirit takes action, it soars like an eagle with supreme strength over the Hot Sulfur Springs. The spirit is the essence of inner strength fueled by the grace of love. Just as the eagle cannot soar without its feathers, a grieving spirit is helpless without God's merciful love.

One of the patterns in Ricky's memorial quilt was his personal sacrifice to fly alone. The fabric of this particular scene in Ricky's life is set in a challenging course of twists and turns along a stretch of highway between the cities of Denver and Colorado Springs in Colorado referred to by the local weather forecasters and traffic reports as Monument Pass. The high point along this stretch of the interstate road is the mountain pass or Monument Hill. Like any mountainous terrain, Monument Pass offers views ordained by nature's beauty such as the view of Pikes Peak. Ricky often told me this pass was the most dangerous part of his drive to and from work. He spoke of the commute with dread and defeat. Yet he was destined to face the road every day. The first time I drove the infamous Monument Pass I did not understand how the road could be so daunting because approaching it from the north, the first impression of the road is a long stretch of straight asphalt and dotted white lines. However, it soon became obvious that the road had the potential to throw a curve at you faster and more furious than the starting pitcher at an All-Star baseball game. The driver's focus could not be distracted less something unfortunate happen. The most important lesson I learned about Monument Pass was not about how to navigate the treachery of the road but how to appreciate the natural changes in its path. Like spiritual growth, the road is not always long and straight as the road conditions change from time to time. Distracted eyes can deter from the path of righteousness into a tumultuous terrain. Straying is inevitable. We learn and become better from making the wrong choice or a bad decision. More importantly, we are wiser from the experience when we get back on the right road again.

Ricky told me whenever he was traveling south on Monument Pass, he felt like he was on the final road that would take him home forever. Sadly, my home was in the opposite direction, miles and miles away. I drove through Monument Pass several times just so I could sit at Ricky's gravesite in hopes of feeling closer to him. Each trip became more onerous and I began to worry that the time would come when I could not make the journey to be with him. Every time I left his gravesite, I could feel my weary heart fall apart from the loneliness I felt from losing Ricky. It was as if one of my spiritual wings were being ripped from my soul. My heart plummeted with the notion that someday I would have to stop visiting Ricky's gravesite because the frame of my body would be too worn and weak to make the drive. I appealed to the empathy of my soul for an answer to my sorrow. The answer was obvious. I did not have to make the drive across the Pass to be with Ricky. Ricky could be with me in Denver.

In Ricky's memory, I designed a memorial garden in my backyard populated with a variety of perennials and annuals as well as garden ornaments and accents. One of my favorite designs was a series of succulents in the shape of a heart. The genesis of the garden, located outside of the flowerbed, was a large circle made of 28 gray landscaping cement stones. Within the circle I positioned a combination of decorative glistening white rock in the shape of the wings of an Angel and four red flat steppingstones in the shape of a cross. In the circle's core was a flourishing purple Larkspur. The garden's peaceful and colorful palate magically delivered me to a state of paradise and immense serenity. I could sit in my garden as long as I wanted and feel like I was not alone. In the sacred confines of nature's cradle, my garden provided the solace I felt when sitting at Ricky's gravesite.

It was common for Ricky and me to try and create things together. There always seemed to be a story in whatever we created like the time we made our wedding rings with two braided, rubber bands and aluminum foil. In hindsight, the rings were significantly more meaningful. Natural rubber is extracted from the Hevea Brasiliensis, better known as the Rubber Tree, when the silver bark is removed. In its purest form, the rubber from this tree is a milky white sap and is nature's unique material for keeping things intact. The inner circle of my wedding ring was a band that held the contents of everything Ricky and I were together. Unlike traditional wedding rings made with precious metals of shining silver or glittery gold, my ring was resilient and would not break when stretched but would return to its original shape. My ring's strength was tested when Ricky's life was taken from me. Like my heart, my wedding ring stretched to its maximum, but it did not snap. Death physically took Ricky away from me but could not take him away from my heart. Our love survived the virtual band holding us intact.

I buried our wedding rings in the circle of my memorial garden. The circle was a powerful source of healing for me as it represents our sacred life together where the many paths of my healing started to grow. Whenever I needed spiritual comfort, I would meditate in the tranquility and beauty of my garden. At times, I walked around the circle moving slowly from brick to brick forward and backward just to remember. Each brick was a memory, a feeling, a prayer, a song and each brick brought me one step closer to understand spiritual harmony and balance. My heart rested on looking back and remembering special times when life was simple and free.

Life behaves in serendipitous ways. I was staying at my Mother's house on the hill, recovering from a concussion after being hit in the head by an airbag in a car accident. I was sitting at a table in what was once my Grandmother's kitchen facing the twin windows that framed the entry to the west. It was early July and the heat from the setting sun gave a preview of the dry balmy days of summer. While researching new landscaping ideas to add to my garden, I glanced down at a torn piece of paper with my birthdate written on it. Staring curiously at each number my eyes moved across each digit one by one from right to left and then left to right. While holding the paper in my hand I reflected on different feelings of grief. Quite possibly, the non-conventional stage of grief is just to feel it. Suddenly, I felt a light breeze lift the heaviness from the nape of my neck. When I was able to lift my head, I opened my eyes to examine my birthdate again on the piece of paper I was holding. For a moment, I wondered if there was something more in my past that I needed to restore. Continuing in my search for new landscaping ideas a link to a Crow Indian legend appeared and caught my attention.

It was as if someone handed me a story of a legend that was dormant and pleaded to bring it back to life and of course I did. I listened to the drumming beat of my heart and I started writing. I began to mend the Crow Indian legend with the threads of my life, the sound of my spirit, the breath of my soul. As I wrote the constant ache that once filled my heart softened. I began to understand why Ricky's death should never live inside my heart. The love that flowed in his veins also flowed in mine. Immune to the temperature outside, I placed my fingers on the keyboard and I transformed the legend into my own personalized narrative. Like a needle making its way through alternating warp threads, I introduced Ricky into the weave by adding the story of our life into the legend's loom.

With the influence by my sacred ancestry, my heart mended a new story...

There is a quiet place on the earth where the world sits still and calm, almost motionless and the place is close to God. The place is called

Villahermosa and is the home of the beautiful people. Villahermosa looked like an authentic diamond on a giant ring that wrapped all the way around the earth. In its stillness, Villahermosa was full of light and overflowing with the sweetness of love. The people that inhabited Villahermosa were amicably kind and most sincere. Clearly, this was not because of what they owned for they possessed very little, but because when they were born they were branded by the nobility of love. The unique mark of this branding was like a magical imprint inside their heart that showered them with a profound eminence of amazing grace, reputed honor and Divine dignity throughout their entire life. The imprint was indestructible. In this quiet place of peace, love was in great abundance.

Villahermosa was adorned with majestic mountain peaks. The crest in the highest mountain looks like a widow's peak shimmering in the sun's golden light. When the ivory white clouds slowly slip down from the face of the sky they appear as if to part the hairline of God so He can shepherd over His people in the Village below. Each morning before the sun begins its ascent the people would awaken and run into the open fields to greet the morning sun. It was truly a blessing for them to join and give thanks for a new day of life. Life in Villahermosa was not a busy place, but everyone worked and shared the virtue of being a hard worker, for they learned early in life, if it wasn't worth working for it wasn't worth having. Everyone shared the virtue of nurturing their mind, spirit, and body with the elements of the earth to keep their love strong and vibrant. Despite its impressive quality of love, the most spectacular aspect of Villahermosa was what covered it. Villahermosa was shrouded by the sheer canopy of a Great Spirit. Under the canopy was an extraordinary sensation of life that illuminated in all colors. Love reflected endless happiness and total joy. This feeling even made you tingle. The brightness of this greater light made you feel complete, as if you were bathed in purity. The light was a gift for everyone and offered an insight into one's higher self. In Villahermosa breathing the light into your inner being was a way to heal the spirit and restore the soul.

Villahermosa, was rooted against the slope of Bighorn Mountain. On the western side of the mountain lived a very handsome young man by the name of Nicho. Nicho had the finest attributes. He was the color of a blushing pearl and was muscular and slender for his height. The women of Villahermosa adored him. Nicho delighted his elders because he loved to talk and engage them in conversation. When the conversations ended Nicho left his elders with inspiring affection and the utmost respect. The elders savored every moment of listening to Nicho because Nicho's spirit had a bright freshness and an inviting innocence to it which was very captivating.

It goes without saying the children were enamored with Nicho too. They clumsily tried to imitate him while stepping inside his big footprints. Nicho always sensed the children near him. He maintained a watchful eye for their safety and the safety of the people of Villahermosa. Because the people of Villahermosa always felt Nicho's electrifying spirit, they loved him even more. This made Nicho smile and when Nicho smiled his smile could surmount the beauty of Villahermosa.

One mystical morning, the sun did not rise, and the sky appeared to be the color of ox blood. That day Nicho seemed especially excited to greet the sun and awoke earlier than the others to properly prepare himself. Not wanting to awaken anyone else, he quietly tiptoed from his bed over to his Mother's stove to boil some water. As the water began to boil, Nicho stared into a red clay pot to admire his beautiful face in the water's reflection. Mysteriously, Nicho lost his balance and fell knocking the pot of boiling water from the stove. A horrific scream echoed over the mountains and throughout Villahermosa. Nicho's Mother awoke startled and smelled the odor of incinerated flesh. She ran to the stove to find her beautiful son in shock, immobilized in pain. His skin was gone, peeled away by scalding water exposing the red, raw muscle. Nicho was burned everywhere; his hands, his arms, his legs, and even his entire face had become covered with blisters. Nicho did not cry aloud but whimpered inside his Mother's arms.

Every sunrise after that fateful morning, Nicho's painful cries disturbed the morning peace and could be heard over the mountains, across the sky, and as far away as the heavens. Because the peace was disturbed the people of the village felt Nicho's pain and stopped greeting the sun in the morning so the sun decided that it would no longer shine. This angered the people of Villahermosa and they slowly lost compassion, patience, hope, trust, and the love that was imprinted in their hearts was fading also away. The people of the village even lost their feelings for others including their family, their home, and ultimately, they lost their virtues.

Nicho's Mother cared for her son's wounds and treated them with a great maternal love. Every day she tried helplessly to make Nicho's scars disappear. Eventually, Nicho started to recover from his burns so that he could function again. He longed to be outdoors with the others, especially to play with the children and talk with the elders. But Nicho was too worried and embarrassed that everyone would see him as a monster. Afraid to show his face, Nicho refused to step outside of his Mother's home. Because Nicho isolated his spirit, his spirit started to weaken like foliage that had been denied water and sunlight. Nicho's grandparents felt badly for him. In their eyes, Nicho was still very beautiful. Every day, his Grandfather would tell him, "Nicho, if you only have one friend by your side then that is all you need!" Nicho carefully listened but did not engage in his Grandfather's wisdom and instead, continued to be alone. Joyful moments in Nicho's life were sparse but Nicho developed a fondness for dancing with his Grandmother. He and his Grandmother danced in the morning as if they were greeting the morning sun. But one day, Nicho became acquainted with death when his Grandmother died and the light of the Nicho's heart faded away. Triggered by his Grandmother's death, Nicho's face worsened. The scars gradually grew darker, longer and larger. The medicine man of Villahermosa told Nicho that the Great Spirit sent a message that Nicho had a very bad condition rooted deep inside his soul that was almost incurable. The Great Spirit called this condition grief.

Nicho hurt everywhere; in his mind, body, spirit and especially deep within his soul just as the Great Spirit had diagnosed. It was a lingering pain Nicho never felt before. He was wounded and very vulnerable. The sun took pity on Nicho. One day with its healing light, the sun found Nicho's spirit and offered an extension of light. In the light Nicho found the courage to face another day and was able to walk outdoors for the first time since he was burned. When Nicho stepped outside he faced a very different cold and cruel world. The Village was not the same. The people of the village were tainted with jealously and greed and the stench of death was everywhere. When the people of the village spotted Nicho, they looked at him with evil in their eyes and hatred in their hearts. In a threatening voice they yelled out to Nicho, "Scarface!" Nicho shunned the people of the village and retreated into his home to be with his Grandfather. Then, like his Grandmother, his Grandfather grew old and died. After Nicho's Grandfather died, the dynamics of his family changed. With the elders gone, there was no respect and the family argued and acted out of jealousy and deceit. Nicho's family started to hate Nicho and when they would get a glimpse of Nicho they yelled out to him, "Burnface!" Nicho knew that the ugliness of the world had seeped into his home and was en route to destroy everything and everyone he once loved. Due to the constant taunting, Nicho decided to flee from his family and his village. He ran to the point of exhaustion and at the highest point of his travels Nicho settled in a place called Medicine Mountain. This mountain was where Nicho could begin to take his first steps to heal the most life threating of his scars; the gash he felt as a result of his spirit being ripped apart from his soul.

Nicho lived on Medicine Mountain where he could take in the smell of pinions and pine. While on the mountain, the Spirits sent Nicho four creatures to teach him different life lessons. Just as a totem pole lies waiting to be sculpted from the tree trunk, hidden within each lesson was an answer waiting to be interpreted by Nicho. One by one the answers, like dissolving sutures placed over the wound, would heal the painful gash inside Nicho's heart. Nevertheless, Nicho had to interpret the lesson to learn the answer.

The first creature to appear to Nicho was a Wolf. The Wolf showed Nicho that light still existed in the darkness of feeling isolated and alone. The Wolf encouraged Nicho to welcome the light of the morning sun back into his life and realize that the darkness is a manifestation of the mind. Fear and uncertainty can disappear if Nicho can see beyond the darkness. The Wolf also told Nicho that he could travel to many beautiful places to relax, find food, and never be seen. Lastly, the Wolf explained to Nicho that Nicho had become a lone Wolf. However, if Nicho were to join others, Nicho must always be the leader and take pride in watching over his pack.

The second creature that was sent to Nicho was a Bear. Nicho was very intimidated by the Bear when it first arrived but quickly realized the Bear was not there to harm him. The Bear taught Nicho the strength of his body and warned him that it was an element of force. Nicho noticed that as large as the Bear was the Bear still appeared soft and gentle and that encouraged Nicho to listen more closely and carefully to the Bear's message. The Bear taught Nicho many things, but the most important lesson was how to hibernate. Whenever Nicho became upset and angry with the Bear, the Bear would tell Nicho, "Go sit in the center of your cave!" When Nicho became frustrated for sitting too long, sometimes the Bear would react and make Nicho sit still and think for an entire season. Only the Bear knew Nicho could find the answers when he sat still; for all answers come from within.

The third creature that arrived was a Buffalo. Unlike the two other animals the Buffalo took his time to reach Nicho. Nicho could see the Buffalo over the hill smelling the roses. It was as if the Buffalo smelled every flower in the pasture. Nicho waited and waited for the Buffalo to join him. When the Buffalo finally reached Nicho, the Buffalo delivered a red pillowcase filled with sweet corn. By that time Nicho was famished. The Buffalo told Nicho, "Whatever you do, do not eat the corn!" Initially, Nicho felt awkward listening to what the Buffalo said because the only thing the Buffalo seemed to do was eat and smell the flowers. The Buffalo managed to get through to Nicho and taught Nicho about enjoying life by working hard. Every day that the Buffalo was in Nicho's life, he made Nicho work. Nicho had to sit down and peel the husks from the corn and separate it into two heaping piles, one for the husks, the other for the corn. Every so often, the Buffalo would look at Nicho with pity because it looked like he was in a corn maze. Every night the Buffalo would then ask Nicho, "Tell me, what did you learn?" For a very long time Nicho only replied, "I am hungry, and this project is pointless!" Nicho even yelled at the Buffalo and said, "I do not want to touch another husk! I do not even know what I am learning!" This disappointed the Buffalo, so he doubled the amount of corn each time Nicho gave him the wrong answer.

As Nicho continued to work separating the husks from the corn into two piles that were growing into small hills all around him, he had plenty of time to be still and think. Nicho learned to quiet his mind and focus solely on his inner feelings. For every second of pain he felt deep inside his wounded heart, he ripped a husk from the corn. He repeated this over and over again until he reached the golden kernels. When he held the stripped corn inside his hands, Nicho gazed at it as if he was looking back at a reflection of golden memories when his life was perfect. Holding the corn and then graciously placing it on top of the pile gave Nicho a sense of welcomed contentment. He felt the release of the weight on his soul and realized he was lighter. Nicho looked back at the hill of husks and felt his worries dissipate into the discarded layers that covered the corn. When Nicho's worries disappeared, so did the Buffalo. The Buffalo paved a path on which Nicho could merge back onto the right road of life again.

The last creature to visit Nicho swooped down like a spirit from the sky and did not stay very long. It was an Eagle. The Eagle flew in a circle above Nicho's head then landed on his shoulder and presented Nicho with a feather. In a wise tone that reminded Nicho of the elders of Villahermosa, the Eagle's spirit told him, "As long as your heart is pure, nothing will ever harm you." The Eagle told Nicho to don the feather and to wear it with pride because the feather belonged to the Great Spirit and was awarded to only the deserving for exceptional valor.

Nicho learned that in and of himself, he was incomplete. Nicho learned who his Completer was. He also learned to revere God and all that God had created. The four creatures, the Wolf, the Bear, the Buffalo and the Eagle made a contribution toward Nicho's life. Each of the four Spirits taught Nicho lessons that gave him the answers on how to bring life back to the living and feel love in his heart. After his last lesson, Nicho looked up at the sky above Medicine Mountain. The radiant sun struck him from head to toe with warm rays of bright light and instantly Nicho realized his mind and body were healed and the light of his spirit was returned. Nicho was finally strong enough to face life again and concentrate on healing his heart and restoring his soul.

The day after Nicho experienced his spiritual transformation, a young woman named Manita and her Nana were taking a walk in the Bighorns. Together they ventured up the mountainous terrain to the highest point in search of the most delicious berries. Nana told Manita the berries reminded her of the berries that once grew abundantly in Villahermosa. Nana whispered in Manita's ear, "Do not tell anyone about the berries!" Nana feared the berries would be poisoned if the toxic people of Villahermosa discovered them. They took pleasure in picking the berries and placed the delicate fruits of their labor one by one inside their hand-woven baskets that rested on their hips.

The day turned sour when Manita and her Nana became severely dehydrated from the heat. As they searched for water a torrential storm suddenly raced over the mountain. The downpour came so quickly that Manita was temporarily separated from her Nana. When the storm subsided, Manita and her Nana were disoriented and became lost on the mountain. Several days later, they were still wandering in and out of the mountainside, walking in circles and trying to find their way back home.

Nana grew very tired and weak. Although Manita appeared delicate and fragile like a baby doe that startled easily with the sound of the wind, Manita was actually quite strong and guided Nana to a safe place where Nana could rest. Many nights passed and then one evening a figure appeared in the shadow of their campfire. This shadow flew around them in circles like a beacon in the night then perched itself on a branch. Through the leaves the shadow peaked over at the young girl and her Grandmother and after a few seconds departed as mysteriously as he appeared. That night Manita went to sleep shivering in the cold but awoke the next day covered with a warm wool blanket. Manita was pleasantly surprised with food and water that she and Nana quickly devoured. Manita picked up the crumbs and whistled to the birds but they did not come. So Manita started to sing softly as if she was singing a lullaby to a newborn drifting off to sleep. Manita's singing lured the birds to her. Birds of different species flocked to Manita as if she was the Mother bird. Even a sparrow holding its broken wing tightly to its tiny body hopped over to her feet. In the distance, Nicho smiled as he witnessed Manita's gentle spirit. Miraculously, Manita even warmed Nicho's heart.

Manita and Nana remained on the mountain unable to travel until Nana regained her strength. The food and water continued to appear every morning just before sunrise. One night, Manita decided she would not sleep but would wait for an opportunity to thank the donor. Determined to stay awake, Manita studied the constellation of stars above her. When the moon started to withdraw and the first streaks of color began to paint the horizon, the mysterious shadow appeared. Manita caught a glimpse and knew instantly that the shadow was that of the legendary Scarface she heard about when she was a little girl, and yet, she was not afraid. Scarface stood near the campfire just as it burned its final embers. Then Manita saw his amazing beauty when he stood next to the fading moon. The scars were concealed by the sun's shimmering morning light. Manita noticed that Scarface's strength was bigger than the entire sky and still he appeared gentle like a giant teddy bear. She was intrigued by the magical power of his beauty and the pure essence of love in his spirit. Scarface knelt by Nana to replenish the food and water. That is when Manita reached out with all her courage and touched his face not with her hands but with her lips. Scarface had never felt such an amazing feeling. His scars melted away seeing his reflection in someone else's eyes. He was the beautiful Nicho again! Nicho's physical scars remained but the emotional scars inside his heart seemed to heal completely and he felt the love of home seep back into his heart. Home was a quiet place called Villahermosa. Nicho gazed into Manita's sparkling eyes, they too were overflowing with love. Nicho kissed Manita and the earth's axis shifted. Manita and Nana were anxious to return to Villahermosa. Manita begged Nicho to join them but Nicho did not want to go back. Then Manita made Nicho sit near her favorite tree, a tree that looked like it was turned up and out of the ground. The tree had a branch that hung low where Manita could sit comfortably. This was the same branch Nicho sat on when he first saw Manita. That particular branch, Manita explained to Nicho, was special as it symbolized their life together and Nicho agreed.

Manita was a very quiet person. It was not in her nature to speak against the will of others. Also, women from Villahermosa never challenged men, especially their husbands. But once again, Manita found her courage and confronted Nicho and said, "First of all Nicho, you cannot let any obstacle stand in your way. Second of all Nicho, we are in this together, for life!" Nicho was so surprised to hear such adamant conviction from such a petite person that it made him grin. Nicho listened to every word Manita spoke and gave her a quick scan up and down. When Manita ended her speech, Nicho gave her a quick nod as if to motion in agreement. Knowing how important it was to Manita, Nicho eventually agreed to go back if they were married. The next day, Nana, Manita and Nicho packed their few belongings and headed down the mountain. Nicho was so happy to be married that he picked up Manita and her Nana on his shoulders and carried them all the way back to Villahermosa.

Upon returning to Villahermosa Nicho was quickly spotted by the wicked people of the village, shouting "Scarface! Scarface! Scarface!" Nicho was tormented all over again. The voices grew louder and louder, the taunting was without end. Nicho fell to one knee while covering his ears. Manita felt Nicho's anguish and shouted back at the crowd. The crowd grew angry and retaliated against Manita by throwing rocks at her. Nicho, struggled to stand and rushed to Manita's aid but he was too late. Manita was struck on the left side of her temple with a very large rock. Dazed, Manita stumbled over to Nicho. Nicho felt a gentle touching sensation rest upon his shoulder. He realized there was no pulse in Manita's hand when she fell into his arms. In Nicho's arms she took her last breath and her spirit left the earth.

Nicho's piercing cries were louder than his screams when the boiling water burned his skin. The Sun heard Nicho's cries and became very angry and called out to the Moon, "Stop! Stop giving all of your light to the people of Villahermosa!" The Moon agreed and started a new moon phase, called the Waxing Crescent. In this phase the moon resembled the lunula on the fingernail of the Great Spirit. It was as if the Great Spirit was pointing his right index finger while reprimanding the people of the village, "No! No! Do not behave this way!" Nicho held Manita's lifeless body in his arms. The Sun and the Moon cried and dimmed their light together to pay tribute as Nicho whispered to Manita, "We are for life!"

Nicho rested Manita's lifeless body safely in his arms and ran as far as his legs would take them until they reached Medicine Mountain. During Nicho's journey back home to the mountain, Nicho never let go of Manita. He carried his wife to the highest point of the mountain, higher than where they had first met. When he finally put Manita down directly under the moon, Nicho asked the Great Spirit to bring her back to life. The Great Spirit did not answer his prayers but told Nicho goodness and mercy will follow but Nicho's purpose in life was yet to come. Nicho did not understand. He was confused and unsure of everything. He recalled what the Medicine Man told him after his Grandmother died. The Great Spirit said Nicho's condition was deeply rooted in his soul and his condition was called grief.

Nicho buried Manita at the peak of Medicine Mountain. In her honor he constructed a memorial of the largest mountain stones that reflected an elite blue sparkle in the moonlight and a warn sapphire brown hue in the ray of the morning sun. With each stone Nicho placed on the ground with his work beaten hands he assured Manita that no stone would ever hurt her again. Nicho did this for years and years until one day Nicho placed the last stone in position on the memorial. He took a step back and noticed that he made a big circle of stones around Manita. Just then a flash of energy whipped past Nicho and the sky opened. Directly above his head, Nicho saw many colors; red, orange, yellow, green, blue, indigo and violet. The colors came together in the shape of a ribbon painted like a Spirit against the sky. Nicho wept when he saw the beautiful colors within his reach. He realized he had grown weary and worn from grief. As he wiped away the tears from his eyes, he noticed another colorful ribbon below the first one. Both ribbons were identical and interconnected in beauty. Nicho thought about the real beauty in his life, Manita, and his heart sank while his spirit sobbed. Nicho lost his will to live. He stepped inside the circle and dropped to the ground to blanket Manita's grave with his dying soul. Nicho begged the Great Spirit to take him and reunite him with Manita. This time, the Great Spirit answered Nicho by saying that Nicho had fulfilled his destiny in building Manita's memorial. Then the Great Spirit opened Nicho's heart and brought him acceptance. Suddenly, Nicho's destiny was clear. He was to return his spirit to bring back life to the people of the Villahermosa, his spirit having been recovered, his soul restored. Nicho's journey was complete. He had confidence in his God and in himself. Nicho's Grand Circle was not just a memorial for Manita but served a much greater purpose for the people of the village and beyond. The Medicine Wheel is a circle that displays the many steps in the journey one would take to mend a broken heart. The circle was a symbol of feeling, learning, remembering, and teaching the most powerful lessons of life before it's too late to learn them.

Today, the Fort Smith Medicine Wheel sits high atop a commanding bluff overlooking the Bighorn River in Wyoming. According to the National Park Service of the Bighorn Canyon Park, no one is certain what prompted Scarface to build the Fort Smith Medicine Wheel or why he constructed the circle the way that he did. The connection I felt with the legend is that the medicine wheel provided me with my own spiritual steps that guided me in a journey to feel and comfort my soul.

The journey through grief is whatever the one grieving perceives it to be. My journey was spiritually directed by a firm belief and trust in God. Although I felt that Ricky's death robbed me of a part of my soul, Ricky's death gifted me the conscious memory forever of his life's lessons. It is not meant for me to understand why I had to experience such loss, nor is it meant to be questioned. I learned that every feeling contains a vital lesson that only grief can teach. Quite possibly, the feelings of grief opened my heart. My story may offer compassion to others experiencing a similar loss. My experience may help others understand their feelings of grief and surrender their hearts to ignite love in their lives, almost like putting another log on the fire before the final flame goes out.

There is love in this world if you choose to love. Inherent in every life is the ability to love and be loved. When love is nurtured by the soul, all things are possible including the ability to survive. Acceptance comes from deep within and gives extraordinary power. Acceptance is not saying "This is okay." It is not okay that Ricky died. Acceptance is saying "This is." This is what happened to me because Ricky died. By accepting Ricky's death, seedlings of hope sprouted from my grief like tulips breaking through the earth's spring frost. Ricky always encouraged me to be the very best. In trying to do so, I hope to teach others how to express their feelings of grief and find their own story.

My story is now recorded in this book and the special love shared by two spirits is sealed and bonded together forever within each letter, each word, each line, and each chapter. Ricky always wanted to be the hero in my life. In the end, Ricky was more than my hero. To me Ricky was a legend, someone I will never forget. Inside my heart and within my soul rests a profound peace and without the slightest vibration of a single vocal cord, the breath of my spirit proclaims to the world, "Yes Ricky, Somos 4-Life!"

Those who seek to find "Razones" from deep within their grief will find their special story.

CPSIA information can be obtained
at www.ICGtesting.com
Printed in the USA
LVHW052313290620
659354LV00002B/515